MORE SWINGS THAN ROUNDABOUTS

The Life of Carlos 'Robin' Medina

JOHN WRIGHT

APS PUBLICATIONS

APS Books,
The Stables, Field Lane,
Aberford,
West Yorkshire,
LS25 3AE

APS Books is a subsidiary of the APS Publications imprint

www.andrewsparke.com

CONTENTS

PREFACE

This book is a biography of sorts of Carlos Medina who, under the stage name Robin Medina, was one of the most famous, respected, and sought-after contortionists and roman ring performers of the 20th Century.

One of the many strange things about this book is that, at the time of writing, Carlos is still alive, and the biography was written through information gleaned in discussions with him -sometimes in the way of drunken rambles, sometimes through semi-structured interviews. This ability to talk directly with the subject is a rare gift for any biographer.

This is not a scholarly work and research, where it took place, was limited to internet searches via Google and some general reading around the nature and history of circuses. The majority of the evidence for the story in the biography comes from Carlos himself, substantiated to some extent by the photographs which I have been keen to try and integrate into the text to fill out the story as much as possible. Carlos is not a literary man and so for him a short verbal account, or an old photograph, evokes the lived event which he often seemed unable to grasp was not my event, and so could not have the same significance or meaning to me. Sometimes the quality of the photographs is not good and where this is the case I thought it better to try and give a rough 'verbal' taste of the event rather than nothing at all.

Clearly for a Circus performer the keystone to his achievement is in the performance and sadly, very little, apart from the photographs of Carlos performing, actually remains. He lived in a time when Circuses were on the decline and the hand-held video, or smart phone had not come into being. I have a copy of a video from a performance he gave in South Africa and I have tried to communicate the impact of viewing this as best I can in the relevant section of the book.

This is one man's life, and another man's description of that life, and this necessary remove seems very reminiscent of the people in Plato's cave, who only see a shadow of reality. I do hope the shadow which I have cast is bold enough to be able to reflect the reality of the skill, ability, courage and compassion that is Carlos Medina.

John Wright

Chapter 1

ABANDONED

The small hamlet of Las Dantas consists of a smattering of roughly made, single-storey cottages or pueblos. They are scattered haphazardly around the top of a small spur, which sticks out like a gnarled, bony finger, from the rugged hand of the massive Venezuelan Andes. Located in the Municipality of Bolívar, in Táchira State, in south-western Venezuela, Las Dantas seldom shows up on maps, being home to only a few hundred people, but it is here, in this almost insignificant rural location, that our world-encompassing story has its humble, if turbulent, beginnings.

Located about 800 metres (2625 feet) above sea-level, Las Dantas, wakes to find its early mornings shrouded by a cold, cloudy mist, which hangs over the small settlement like a silent ghost. The mist is soon dispersed, burning off quickly when the first rays of the sun begin to gently caress the rough grass and hard rocky soil on which Las Dantas is built. In late November, that sun-kissed caress soon turns into a relentless assault, as the temperature rises quickly to a hot 25 degrees centigrade. It was into this bright, shimmering heat haze that, on the 25th November 1950, one more, hungry, screaming, boy-child struggled into an unwelcoming world.

Very little is known about the child's mother, except that she was not married to the father. A few days after his birth, she and the child set out on the long arduous journey, up and over the mountainous terrain, heading north-east, across the border-marking-river, Táchira, into Cúcuta, a prosperous Columbian City. Although only about fifty Kilometres away as the crow flies, the lack of roads, the stifling heat, and the scared, hungry, screaming child, would have made the journey both painful and exhausting. Once in Cúcuta, his mother quickly found her way to the home of the man who had wronged her, and unceremoniously left the babe, wrapped in swaddling clothes, on his doorstep, then vanished, never to be heard of again.

It was not until at the age of 18, in a heart-shattering moment of revelation by his paternal grandmother, that the child would learn the truth about his early abandonment. He never met his mother, or indeed ever met anyone from his mother's side of the family. Nor does he have any memory of this painful final journey with her. Her true identity was to remain a mystery for the rest of his life. As he grew up and began to realize that she had abandoned him, so too, he chose to abandon her, never seeking to find her again.

The following day, the angry father, Carlos Alirio Medina-Torres, retraced the mother's steps, and took the child back to Las Dantas. Finding no trace of his one-night-stand, he dumped the child in the local orphanage. Although *orphanage* is probably too grand a word for the small cottage that housed the good Catholic family willing to take in unwanted children.

The good-hearted family were affiliated to an organization known as the 'Congregation for Conclusion' and it was here that the abandoned child was to spend the first three-and-a-half years of his wretched life, sharing what little, food, love and affection there was, with three or four of his equally unwanted young peers.

The following year, 1951, at the instigation of his paternal grandmother, Lola, the child was christened into the Catholic Church and given the name, Carlos Alberto Medina.

Sometime in 1954, at the age of three-and-a-half, whether because he had grown too old, or because there was a demand for the bed, Carlos was transferred from Las Dantas to a sister orphanage located in the San Louis district of Cúcuta. This was a much larger affair, able to care for some eleven or twelve children, but in reality still a small, single-storey cottage, built with hand-pounded adobe-mud walls. Here, the trappings of the Catholic Church were much more manifest, the establishment being run by nuns and a resident priest.

Carlos shared a room with another child and spent his days being indoctrinated into the tenets of the Catholic Church, learning about good and evil, and the endless love of god. Reading and writing were skills the nuns were unable to impart, and it was not until much later in his life that he was able to acquire those. The nuns were strict, but not cruel, in the sense that they never beat him unnecessarily. However, when he misbehaved, or could not recall his catechism, his punishment was to be forced to stare at the wall for twenty minutes - hell on earth to a vital, energetic young boy!

Although Cúcuta was a City of over half a million people at the time, poverty was still the prevailing state of being. Money, and the means of survival were the main issues that occupied everyone who lived in that region. Living off charity meant that life at the orphanage was basic at best. The children lived on a diet of arepa (a soft white bread made from frying or grilling corn - maize - and forming part of the staple diet of Venezuela and Columbian) rice, and vegetables, mainly carrot, cauliflower, and a crudely cooked cabbage dish being a regular 'favourite'. Eggs were an expensive luxury that were only made available once a month. In a coffee producing country, which Columbia was, it seems ironic that coffee was considered too expensive to feed to the natives. Instead, the children lived on a brown coffee-like liquid which was in reality the residual juice produced from adding water to the crushed sugar-cane pulp.

One high spot for Carlos was that his paternal grandmother, Lola, would visit him once a month, and the love-starved child was delighted to accept and rejoice in even this meagre morsel of affection. However, his grandmother's visit also instigated a degree of unpleasantness for the child. Those of you familiar with Spanish nomenclature will note that his name, Carlos Alberto Medina, was rather unusual. The normal procedure with Spanish family names, is for the new family to indicate their origin and celebrate the merging of the two families by sharing a combination of the surnames of the mother and the father. In Spain, there is a specific combination, the father's first surname becomes the child's first surname, and the mother's first surname becomes the child's second surname. However, his mother's name remaining unknown - or too sinful to be revealed- the child was generously given the surname of his paternal grandmother - Medina. When she would visit, the other children at the orphanage would mock him, asking in the cruel taunting way only children can, that if his surname consisted of only his grandmother's name, how could his grandmother also be his mother?

Although, his grandmother's visits produced a bittersweet experience for him, a real and very significant moment of joy, in this otherwise bleak lifestyle, was the regular visit of the circus. It was established practice among touring circuses to extend their benevolence to the local orphanages. They clearly could not afford to transport the children from the orphanage to the circus, which would usually have been set up in some central location in the town or city, so the protocol was to send their 'apprentice' performers to the orphanage, where they could hone their skills further, under the adoring eyes of the eager and often over-appreciative children.

It was on one such visit when Carlos was about five or six that he got his first glimpse of a potential road to freedom. A thin, shy, young girl had arrived with the other performers and was lurking in the background awaiting her turn to 'step into the light'. Eventually she was pushed forward and to everyone's amazement began to contort and bend her slim, lithe, little body in seemingly unbelievable ways. To gasps of amazement and loud applause she contorted into what looked like excruciating positions; lifting her legs behind her neck, or lying on the dusty ground and effortlessly bending her back until she was able to rest her ankles beside her ears.

Carlos was hooked. He had always been a supple child but after witnessing his first contortionist act, he began to consciously work on bending his body, and stretching his flexible back into more and more extreme positions. Suddenly, like many children of his age only dream of doing, the idea of running away to join the circus seemed more like a plausible possibility. However, it was to be some way off before it became a reality, and in the mean-time he made himself content with stretching and bending for his own satisfaction.

Although his time at the orphanage had not been a happy one, he had lived through it, and he only had one major, final indignation to endure. At the age of six and a half, he was to suffer, what has subsequently been revealed to be a seemingly lasting tradition of the Roman Catholic Church. The priests were normally resident at the orphanage for a year or two before moving on to new pastures. Earlier in the year a new priest, Father Biachi, had arrived to take up his spiritual role as head of that somewhat dysfunctional orphan family. The father had singled Carlos out and seemed keen to secure him a place in heaven, by having him able to recite his catechism to such a level of perfection that would make even God himself proud. To enable him to do this he insisted that Carlos join him in the small dusty 'study' at the back of the building at about one o'clock most afternoons. At this time, in the constant, cloud-free heat of the day, the other occupants of the orphanage would take a sensible siesta, sleeping through the worst of the heat. Instead of choosing sleep and comfort, Father Biachi, chose to teach Carlos in this silent and deserted time. It began innocently enough with the Priest praising and stroking him gently on the head and arms and rewarding him with a treat of strong, dark, bitter tasting indigenous cocoa. However, as time went on the Father grew more adventurous, caressing his thick black hair, touching his cheek, and stroking the boy's legs. Eventually his hands strayed further ending up fondling the boy's childish genitals. Soon he went so far as to penetrate him with his crude stubby finger, and to perform fellatio upon him, all in the name of the Catechism. This abuse at the hands of his substitute 'father', who was meant to protect and watch over him, went on for over a year and probably would have continued had not the machinations and complexities of the law intervened.

In Venezuela and Columbia, the law maintains that an orphaned child can be cared for by the state until the age of six, but must then be returned to the family. So, much later than normal, at the age of seven-and-a half, through force of legal necessity, Carlos was finally collected from the orphanage by his grandmother and taken to live with his paternal family.

He was an unwanted guest in this already bustling household, and was forced to share a room with his grandmother, Lola, who had already been so generous in sharing with him her family name. She was a deeply religious woman, and Carlos would watch her in the shadowy, dusty bedroom, reciting her prayers and counting her beads, like a woman desperate for atonement.

It was here too, in the small single-storey family home, that he first met his great-grandmother, Eloise, and he was left in no doubt that these dourly strict adults considered him as one more unwanted burden in their already overburdened lives. The home was held together by the valiant efforts of Lola, who, not content with having had to bring up her own child, was now destined to bring up her flagrantly promiscuous son's unwanted offspring too.

In this poverty stricken home it also appeared that hatred and meanness were the only 'virtues' that were ever to be manifest. To say there was no love lost would be something of an understatement. Home for Carlos was to evoke a memory of oppressive heat, cattle, mosquitoes and a pervading sense of lovelessness, poverty and hatred.

Carlos' father, Carlos Alirio Medina-Torres, had been born in Cúcuta, and was a cobbler by trade, making shoes from leather, tanned from the local cattle. Plying his trade in the family home, he had little time for this, the latest fruit of his loins, and Carlos was to receive no love or kindness from him.

His grandmother, Lola Medina-Torres, sold lottery tickets in the market square. Lola was about 54 years of age when Carlos moved in, and her mother, Carlos' great-grandmother, was about 78. His great-grandmother had the unusual profession of monumental mason - sculpting gravestones. It was she who would carve the names of the dead, and their carefully worded tributes, into the hard unforgiving stone or marble tombstones; helping those who had passed beyond to achieve, in some small way, their vain wish to outlive their allotted brief lifespan on this ever-renewing earth. Strange though her profession was, it seemed to Carlos to somehow enhance her uniqueness. The esteem, reverence and awe that Carlos felt towards Eloise seemed to greatly outdo that which he felt for Lola. A devout Catholic, she was a woman of few words, but when spoken, her words seemed to shake heaven and earth with their prophetic wisdom. Even today Carlos speaks of Eloise with deference, quoting things she said and illustrating them as they have come to pass in the modern world. The shadows and mysteries of death, life and the Roman Catholic Church, wrapped their heavy dark cloak around him, almost shrouding this insignificant hapless little child.

Considered as but yet another mouth to feed, Carlos quickly learned to make himself as invisible as possible.

He was painfully unhappy. Having been rejected at birth by his mother and abused by the substitute family of the church who took him in, here he was yet again being cast off and ignored by his real family.

He amused himself by practicing his new found art of contortionism, bending and stretching his body until he was supple and flexible and able to imitate the positions he had first seen that young circus performer adopt. With no school to contain him, he would sometimes wander away from the family home and saunter off into the woods picking up the sweet, ripe guavas that had fallen from the trees or playing with the wild guinea pigs, or sitting by the banks of the Rio Táchira watching for hours the small silver fish darting and flashing in the shallow waters below, dreaming of a world in which he was wanted, loved, adored and applauded.

Chapter 2

NEW HOME! NEW FAMILY!

Carlos was a precocious child; he was also very tenacious. The image of the lithe little girl and her extraordinary contortions had stayed with him like a vision. Often, sitting in the cool, stuffy, gloom of his Grandmother's house, while the adults took their siesta, he would think of her. She was an angel of hope, a way out of his wretched condition and represented a vibrant golden brick road to a bright rainbow future.

The current reality was somewhat different. Life at home continued to be difficult and the fact that he was an unwanted guest was never allowed to slip from his mind. Some days he was happy, playing with imaginary friends and enjoying the simple pleasures of life in the way only children can. However, he still found the heat of the plains stifling. The hot air was laced with the throat-grasping stench of cattle, and the endless buzzing of angry flies made even the physical surroundings of his life unpleasant.

However, with his now new-found purpose in life he would spend some time each day bending, stretching and twisting himself into seemingly impossible positions in an effort to emulate his one true friend - his inspiring angel! His twisting and bending exertions enlisted only further scorn, contempt and derision from his disapproving father.

Time crawled by in this lacklustre manner, until at the ripe old age of nine Carlos decided to step forward and take charge of his own life, determined to change it forever. The Circus continue to visit Cúcuta, normally around Christmas and Carlos had contrived, via his soft-hearted Grandmother, to visit the show whenever they were in town. This year it was the *Royal Dunbar Circus* and during their visit, the pretty, precocious little boy took it upon himself to visit the members of the contortionist act after the show. Not only that, but he informed them he wanted to join the circus, become a member of the contortionist troupe and travel the world with them. He then proceeded to demonstrate his developing contortionist skills. What the Algeciras family made of this strange little boy and his wonderfully brave self-promotion was sadly never recorded.

Returning to the family home later that day the child was beside himself with excitement. Not only had he seen the circus but he had spoken to people who were living his dream. The house was abuzz with a turbulent energy and even the level-headed Lola, the only real family champion the child had, seemed to have been infected more than usual with the enthusiasm and audacity of her young charge. Strangely too, the excited talk seemed to have affected even his father, Carlos senior, for he showed an uncharacteristic interest in the boy's delight, asking about the circus, the name of the troupe, where they were from, and how long they were likely to be in town for?

Clearly, somewhere at the back of his father's mind a small seed was being nurtured of the possibility, that no matter how seemingly unlikely, these unsuspecting circus folk might be a way to rid himself of his unwanted charge.

However, Carlos was oblivious to this developing diabolical plot. He was still bathing in the joy of recalling his talk with the circus family, and his brief -

but in his mind wonderful - performance in front of them, showing off his bending and contorting skills. Not all of us have such a clear direction in life, an early sense of purpose, ambition and a goal, but at the age of nine Carlos had successfully managed to steer his life and point it firmly towards a profession and way of life that he thought he loved and wanted for himself. He had somehow managed to twist and contort the conditions of his own life to his own purpose, even if it was to take many more years of hardship for that end to be fully realised.

Later that night Carlos was amused to hear his great grandmother in a state of great anxiety shouting that his father was going to feed him to the lions! The commotion between the women and the man of the house seemed to go on for some time, and raised voices in the adjoining room kept him awake longer than normal that night. Carlos, unable to make out details assumed it was just another family row. He did not for one minute entertain the possibility that the row could be about him. Choosing to ignore the continuing kerfuffle, he turned his back on the noise and eventually fell asleep.

The next morning something clearly was afoot. Lola informed Carlos that they were going to visit the circus again today. Carlos was delighted, but rather puzzled when she added that his father Carlos Senior would also be coming with them.

After the show, Carlos and Lola, with Carlos Senior in tow, retraced their steps of the day before and approached *Las Truppe Algeciras*. Once again Carlos spoke of his passion for contortionism and demonstrated, yet again, the current abilities of his lithe and supple young body. The Algeciras again seemed

14

impressed, but this time the whole event took a markedly different turn.

Standing in the cool, dark interior of the cathedral-like canvas of the big top, Carlos senior began to spell out the fine print and details of a Faustian deal. However, unlike Faust who sells his own soul to the devil, Carlos senior was not about to sell his soul to these circus devils, but rather that of his son: and not just his soul, but his body too. It must have been an odd and unnatural negotiation. Here was a man, with his own mother standing beside him, and in full view of the child he was talking about, declaring that he was willing to sell his own flesh and blood, his young, nine-year old boy to a family he had never met before. From his point of view, it was perfect; for, in one fell swoop, he would be ridding himself of an expensive burden, and coming away with a handsome profit for his troubles. With no safeguards, or conditions of care built into the contract, a deal was rapidly struck, and unceremoniously, in that quick verbal exchange the father had sold his son into the circus for the princely sum of thirty American dollars - about $200 at today's prices!

The pain, grief, desolation and anger that Carlos felt cannot be described. In a life already overfull with acts of betrayal, abandonment and suffering here was yet one more act of inhuman cruelty, perpetrated by his own flesh and blood, his own father! The hurt of this moment was to remain with Carlos for the whole of his life.

Chapter 3
THE CIRCUS FAMILY

The next day, as the crew sweated and strained in the background dismantling the big top, Carlos was taken by the distraught Lola and the wailing Eloise, to be fed to the Lions, in the shape of the circus director, Senior Salida Mer Megeu Ruggely, the man who so eagerly and willingly paid out thirty US dollars for the boy, as if buying an apple or any other common item at a simple peasant market. Carlos was in agony with feelings of fury and hatred for his real father, which were never really to subside, and feelings of fear, anxiety and terror towards the new and unknown future. He boarded the bus and sat by the window in wonder and worry, and waved keenly to Lola and Eloise as it pulled out of the hot, dusty bus station, heading for the next town which featured on that year's circus tour.

During this journey Carlos met and learned about the members of his new 'Circus Family'. The family consisted of a 'mother'(Sanidad) and 'father' (Los) along with three girls, Sonia (aged fifteen), Marelleni (aged seventeen), and Alcedia (aged twenty-two) and a boy called Maneco who was about fifteen at the time. As the children were all older than Carlos, they were already well trained in the skills of circus performing, and had been part of the show that Carlos had visited the day before.

Now on this strange unexpected journey together, the girls took time to fuss over the sweet, new family member; the precocious little child, who only the day before seemed eager to show off his own skills and abilities. Meanwhile the boy, Maneco, who was going through the turmoil and pain of adolescence, seemed completely indifferent to this new arrival. Carlos soon realised to his relief that the circus family wasn't very strict. He was free to do as he wished on the bus and, apart from some occasionally fussing by the girls, no one took very much notice of him. The adults seemed perfectly happy to let the children be children and leave them to their own devices.

However, as the bus rattled and groaned down the bumpy uneven roads, he came to learn another more sinister piece of knowledge. In the eyes of the world the circus director's family appeared as a happy, normal family, but in reality they were nothing of the sort. None of the four children travelling with him were his. They, like Carlos, had all been purchased from impoverished families, as Senior Los had travelled across South America. Families who were only too eager to rid themselves of a hungry child, who they had come to see as merely an extra mouth to feed, in exchange for some 'pieces of silver', by which, in the short term at least, they could feed their own hungry mouths.

Later, Carlos was to realise that all the children in the family were being exploited. To his circus father, Carlos was to be nothing but a source of revenue. He was soon to be taught a trade and a highly specific set of skills, which were to build on his own already established childish abilities, in order that he could be put to work to earn the gratitude or reward of the only god that his circus father served – money!

It was odd to think that this small child now heading across the rough roads of Columbia, in a rickety old bus was about to join a very famous tradition. A tradition that many children once used to dream about joining -

that of the Circus. No doubt the dreams Carlos cherished while watching the fish darting to and fro in the silvery Rio Táchira, and the images that rose in his mind after seeing his first 'angel like' contortionist were unlike the bizarre reality that he currently found himself within. When he was older he would be able to look back and see that his particular entry into the world of the circus was no more strange or unusual than that made by other friends. As he became more established in the world of the circus, many tales of shady deals, and surreptitious sales, were to reach his ears.

Interestingly enough, the credit of having created the very first circus way back in 1768 normally goes to a former English cavalryman, a certain Sergeant-Major Philip Astley (1742-1814). Astley was a skilled horseman, who began by performing tricks on horseback at his riding school near Westminster Bridge in London. The main form of entertainment at that time was the Theatre, and Astley's shows were considered an extension of that. He performed his feats of wonder in a circular arena that he called the *circle*, or *circus,* a shape he had borrowed from other performers whom he had seen on his travels. The circle, circus, or circus-ring as it has finally come to be called, had proved a very expedient shape for performers, as it enabled the audience to keep the riders fully in their sight throughout their entire performance. Additionally, previous riders performing in this way, had discovered that riding in a circle helped to generate a centrifugal force which enabled them to maintain their balance while they stood on the backs of their galloping steeds.

At that the time, Astley's performances were very much in demand, and he soon began to add new and more exotic 'acts' to embellish his shows; employing strong men, acrobats and even clowns. The circus, as we now know it today, had well and truly been born from Astley early experiments. One of the great assets and enduring qualities of the circus is that it is essentially a visual performing art, and therefore unfettered by any language barriers, so, without need of any complex translation apparatus, it was able to travel freely all over the globe. When Carlos was finally able to take his place with Las Truppe Algeciras he would become another wonderful, yet silent, addition, to the mystery, excitement, thrill and pleasure that is the circus. But first there was some work to be done.

A very old joke has it that contortionists are the only people who can make both ends meet. To be a contortionist requires a very high degree of physical fitness, muscular control and flexibility of the human body. Over the years there has been a high degree of fear and prejudice around contortionists, considering them to be freaks of nature. The colourful title "India rubber man" seems to bear witness to the belief that they are somehow mysterious and exotic.

Despite claims to the contrary contortionists are not double-jointed, or even mysterious, but devoted performers who have worked very hard to become supple and flexible enough to be able to contort or bend into positions that otherwise look unattainable. They are referred to as 'benders' in the profession and as performers they not only have to get into awkward, and seemingly impossible positions, but also to present those poses in an artistic, graceful, attractive and effortless looking manner.

In Carlos's case the training was arduous. When the family finally completed their Columbian tour during which Carlos had become the newest family member they moved on to tour Peru. The family did not own a house, or a caravan, but lived in hotels, and seemed to spent their entire year touring the length and breadth of South America, with a variety of different circuses. So, now fully part of that itinerate family, Carlos got used to living in cheap hotels and moving on regularly, and slowly began to learn the skills necessary to master his new profession.

Training began at eight thirty in the morning and continued until about eleven thirty when there would be a break for lunch. It would then resume again after the adult's siesta around two thirty and continue until about five thirty each and every day. Carlos was to train in this manner from the age of nine until he was thirteen years old.

The body does not naturally bend into the unusual positions that form the mainstay of the contortionist's act and the bulk of the training consisted of the child being pushed and held in these sometimes painful positions by someone else until his bones and muscles had become supple enough to accommodate this new pose. To be a successful contortionist requires highly skilled support, someone who has the talent to squeeze and shape you into the exotic positions required. If they do not have the necessary talent one could end up disabled or deformed. Luckily for Carlos, his newly acquired 'Circus Mother' was the person skilled at manipulating him during the long daily training sessions. She was a professional contortionist as well as being a dislocator and it was she who was to supervise and direct all his strenuous training. Dislocation is different from contortionism. Contortionists are able – through extensive and systematic training - to make their body supple and pliable, whereas dislocators, as the word implies, actually dislocate their joints in order to squeeze into otherwise seemingly impossible positions.

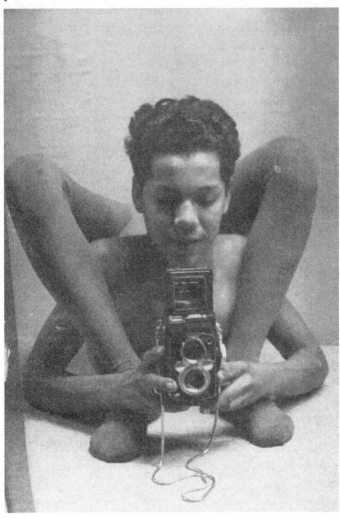

Carlos trained outdoors and, because he was still growing, his cartilage was changing all the time which meant that he had to be continually trained and re-trained to stretch the new and ever-expanding tissue. As the family was constantly travelling and performing in different towns and cities across the length and breadth of South America his exertions took place in a variety of sights and settings. Mostly they were outside in the warm sustaining air of the plains, where his main prop was a coconut tree, against which he pushed and stretched and raised his short young legs, doing battle against his muscles and growing sinews. Sometimes he struggled in the more refined high-altitude air of the mountains, looking out over breath-taking vistas. But all the time he was stretching, twisting and bending, holding poses until his supple little body felt it would break under the strain, and all this in addition to the even longer and more painful periods when his 'mother' manipulated and forced his pliable young form into new and unusual positions.

For the young boy suddenly to be bathed in this constant and meaningful attention was like being lifted into a new realm, far, far away from the darkness and lonely sadness of his former home. Although, the shame of being sold and cast out of his family by his own father, was a constant thorn buried deep in his young flesh to which he returned with fury from time to time, on the plus side, in response to all this attention, Carlos proved a hard-working and devoted pupil, striving to attain even the most seemingly painful and impossible positions. His young limbs were up for the challenge and that distant radiant image of the young angelic girl which first inspired him continued to draw him ever onward.

It was not just the children who trained, the adults too went through their moves and performances, keeping their bodies and minds agile. After the mornings limbering and the light lunch of arepas and fruit the adults would settle down for a traditional siesta. The children, being considered too young and active to require a siesta, would engage in another skill; that of creating bead jewellery. The outcomes of this art were used to good effect in enhancing their costumes by creating dazzling and sparkling effects which under the bright floodlights of the big top would make the performers seem even more exotic. Carlos would sit in the cool, stuffy, gloom of the hotel room with his adopted brother and sisters, skilfully making the bead embroidery with his dexterous young fingers. Threading together a range of vibrant and sparkling colours and shaping them into wonderful abstract patterns or, with more effort, fashioning them into images of flowers, animals, or pictorial representations depicting pastoral scenes. It was normal for Circus performers to make their own costumes. Later in his career, by using the skills learned as a child through making the bead embroidery, Carlos was able to add a colourful, sparking and flamboyant flare to the otherwise rather drab dyed cloth of his basic circus togs.

His new family, although providing the basic necessities of life, and at a much higher level that Carlos had experienced before, were also very professional about what they wanted him to learn and know. They were prepared to take a long-term view of their investment and were keen to ensure that Carlos was not exposed to the wild world of the performance until he was completely ready. While the family was on tour with a circus, Carlos was not involved in the performance, and the training regime was somewhat relaxed. He was only required to practice four or five hours per day not the usual nine. This was considered sufficient to keep him flexible and loose. His daily efforts were not to show fruit until the ripe old age of eleven-and-a-half when he was allowed to step into the ring for the very first time.

Carlos was not only trained to be a contortionist but also to perform his contortionism high up on the Roman Rings. These would sometimes be situated as high as 30 feet off the ground. He also learned how to be a dental contortionist, hanging by his teeth while spinning or bending into exotic and extravagant shapes. It was while practicing his dental contortionism that Carlos had his first fall. His sister Alcedia, who was helping him master this technique, was holding him by the neck, while Carlos was supporting his body by only his teeth. When he was in position, Alcedia asked him if he was okay, and he foolishly replied yes, thereby letting go of his grip and falling sharply to the ground. Luckily, he was unharmed apart from some light bruising and a dented pride. He very quickly learned the lesson 'don't speak while you are holding yourself up by your teeth' and never repeated that mistake.

Part of the strictness of the training involved being kept away from other children and their frivolous and childish games. He was forbidden from playing with them. This was not a form of punishment but an expedient means to help keep his mind focussed and concentrated. Playing with other children was considered bad for concentration. For a contortionist distraction was a deadly vice. A momentary lapse in concentration could mean a fatal fall from the high-wire, or from a ring. So, he, and the other children in his newly found family, had to endure this strict regime to enable them to keep their minds fully focussed on their training and devoted to improving their skills.

This strict disciplined approach was to last well beyond childhood, so great was the need for concentration (or fear of the consequences of distraction) that even in adulthood it was a rule that while the show was running he was never to spend time or meet up with people before performances. Although it may seem overly restrictive, this rule was less arduous to observe in practice than it may at first seem. Eventually, when he was a fully trained performer Carlos would perform two shows a night one at six-thirty and another at nine-thirty. On a Saturday they would perform three shows a day and on a Sunday four! Thus the conflict between performance and a burgeoning social life was never really an issue. Being a circus performer was a serious profession, and the role of the young apprentice was very much respected. In those days one was expected to have trained for many, many years before one ever got anywhere near a public performance!

Chapter 4

THE FIRST PERFORMANCE

From the age of nine until he was twelve Carlos kept up the rigorous training regime, worked hard and devoted himself to learning the skills necessary to be able to perform at the highest possible level of achievement. With his circus family he travelled all over South America, visiting large towns and cities as well as many small and remote communities who seemed starved of culture and entertainment and who were only too delighted to break from their daily toil to witness the marvels and wonders that the circus revealed to them.

The circus is very traditional in South America. Indeed, for a long time it was probably the only or main form of available entertainment. His family could spend a whole year travelling around and never visit the same place twice. For example, the Republic of Colombia, a country smaller in area than the North American state of Alaska, in 1970 had a total population of about twenty million people, and these twenty million people were spread across the country, some in the very large cities like Bogota, the capital, which had a population of over two million; Barranquilla with a population of over one million, and Cartagena with a population of about half-a-million. The family could easily spend a whole year performing in Colombia alone. While they were touring it was normal to spend between three to four weeks in each location, obviously longer in a very large city.

Despite the daily proximity to each other, the relationship between family members was almost entirely professional in nature. There was never any real warmth or affection shown between the adults to the children, or between the children themselves. Although there was a fondness and the bond that constant proximity provides, there was little real love or concern. Each was out to meet their own selfish needs and wants whatever these might be. As he had witnessed on that first prolonged encounter on the bus he was free to do what he wanted, as long as it did not detract from the training. There was no sharing of gifts at Christmas time and birthdays came and went and were only noteworthy when the increase in age meant that legislation impacted on them in the shape of requirements for visas or passports or in some other aspect of state officialdom.

After his father sold him to the circus, Carlos had very quickly learned his first hard lesson in life, that he would have to learn to look out for himself. These people were not his real family. There was no natural friendship between them. He soon learned that if you wanted something as simple as a cup of tea, you made it yourself, and so this attitude of self-preservation and selfish gratification was the dominant modus operandi of his formative years. The adults in this family were not looking for love; they were only interested in making money. The only time they spent together was out of necessity in order to train.

It was as if love had died within him, or rather had been murdered by the cruelty of those who should have cherished and nurtured him. From now on, it seemed as if he was tasked with carrying the corpse of Love around within him, hidden deep in his heart, yet always keeping one eye open to the world in the hope that someday a prince charming would come along, flesh it out and then kiss this brittle skeleton back to life.

27

The whole family were all very individualistic and equally indifferent to each other and there was little spoken communication between them. A normal day for Carlos was just practice, practice, practice. Having spent his day twisting and contorting his poor little body until the pain was almost overwhelming, at night his poor little heart and mind would contort together tying him up in emotional knots as he experienced, in short painful waves the pain of desertion, betrayal and the overwhelming desolation which resulted from the lack of being loved. This would peak in feelings of rage, bitterness, fury, and anger and run riot for a while until exhaustion dragged him down into the shadowy world of sleep where his dreams, in their mysterious, chaotic, and irrational manner, would find some way to unravel and straighten out the kinks, so that by the morning, he was able once again to face the day anew.

During his whole time with them, his circus father Los and he exchanged very few words and when they did it was all about the craft. "Practice, practice, practice." he would say or, "Do it again. Repeat it again." This was the sum total of their relationship. The family never had a social life. Indeed, they were not allowed to have one. The adults didn't want the children to talk or socialize with other people, so when the older sister and the mother and father were having a siesta in the early afternoon, the younger ones were left sewing, and repairing costumes safely hidden away from normal social intercourse.

Of course, despite this lack of direct communication, living very closely with other people, one comes to learn about them in ways that are often unconscious and unexplained. One is constantly observing, assessing and anticipating their behaviour, based on the way they behaved before in similar circumstances, and consequently one anticipates that they will behave in such a manner again if a similar situation arose. All this 'unconscious' information is stored away in one's brain often without one even being aware of it. If asked about someone, one would be hard pressed to articulate what one knew: however, intuitively, one knows quite a lot about the people one is constantly surrounded by. For a performer this chthonic intuitive knowledge is important if not crucial, especially when one's life is in the hands of the other person, but as a means of building normal human family ties it is sadly wanting.

As Carlos entered his twelfth year he had been with the family for three years and they had all grown up a little in the intervening time. Sonia was now seventeen, Marlene was twenty-one and Alcina, the oldest, was about twenty-five. The only other boy, Maneque, who was about eighteen, was showing signs of restlessness. Carlos had always considered that Maneque, who was older than him, was also cleverer, and braver and it came as no surprise to Carlos a few years later when Maneque, who had come to realise he was gay, escaped from the shackles of such a constraining regime and ran away to live out his own life in the way that he wanted.

During these years of practice and constant travel, Carlos had also been an observer, watching closely as the family entered the ring, absorbing - by osmosis - the adulation and the applause directed at them, but also watching critically, in the sense of one seeking to learn from their abilities and skills as they went through their highly proficient and impressive routines. Soon all this was to change.

In 1962, the same year that the world watched in fear, horror and trepidation as the Cuban Missile Crisis began to unfolded; that Marilyn Monroe was found dead after apparently overdosing on sleeping pills and the Beatles released their first hit single *Love Me Do*, the twelve year old Carlos had more important issues on his mind. He had been informed that he would be allowed to perform with the family as a full member of the troupe later in the year.

At long last, all the training, discipline, and hardship had led to this one pinnacle of opportunity and now seemed worthwhile. Suddenly the search was on for a stage name. As in other forms of public entertainment no one in the world of the circus used their real names, tending to beg, borrow or steal exotic sounding names whenever possible. In fact the more exotic the better! It is very common in the world of entertainment for artists to create a new 'stage' personality with a brand new name. The world-famous Marilyn Monroe was actually born Norma Jean Mortenson, and David Bowie was born David Robert Jones and more recently Dylan Kwabena Mills felt the need to change his birth name and adopt the stage name Dizzee Rascal.

For Carlos a change of name was needful too. The Spanish name 'Carlos' means 'manly' so when applied to the thin, lithe figure of the four-foot tall child of this period, it had a somewhat comical and contradictory association. Also, Carlos, was probably one of the most common Spanish names of the time. However, help was at hand in the figure of the very active, acrobatic and heroic, masked crusader. The famous American duo of Batman and Robin were iconic Comic Book heroes of the sixties, and everyone knew of their adventures and heroic deeds.

To his family, the muscular caped figure of the young Robin of the comics (also known as the 'Boy Wonder') seemed a perfect match for the equally muscular, precocious and attractive figure of Carlos. Both 'boys' had black hair, both were energetic and athletic, both were slim (Carlos had a twenty-one inch waist at that time) and the Robin of the comics was used to flying through the air much in the same way that Carlos was to spin high up on the Roman Rings. From the rather bizarre marriage of Comic and Circus the magnificent Robin Medina was born! This match seemed even more heaven-born when a few years later in 1966 a TV series of Batman and Robin was created with actor Burt Ward as Robin while Adam West played Batman.

Complete with his new name, 'Robin' was now ready to step into the limelight for the first time. That season the family was travelling once again with the *Royal Dunbar* circus and in July they arrived in Lima, Peru and it was here that Carlos first ran into the ring to taste the reward for all the effort he had been making for so long. The first performance was of necessity a cooperative effort, and involved the whole family performing together as a troupe.

Unfortunately the only pictures we have of this time are of such poor quality that they can't be reproduced here. However they show the petite figure of Carlos attired completely in white and attentively observing, while other family members go through their paces. The father, Los, also attired in a silky white outfit – though topped off with an elaborate looking turban – stands arms folded, gazing proudly at his talented 'children' under the rather menacing open jawed teeth-baring figure of a clown. Marlene is holding a handstand, feet straight up into the air, while balancing on Sonia's knees, and Alcida stands, hands on hips watching the crowd, watch her.

By way of contrast, in the photograph below we see Carlos centre stage, eyes focused in concentration, adopting a complex reverse bend. He is balancing on the firm strong thighs of Sonia while she too is holding a complex back bend. The father, Los, on the right, is once again looking on, but this time it seems to be a more careful scrutiny, checking the position of the boy and seemingly alert to the possibility of a tumble. Meanwhile, Alcida stands on the left, completing the picture and smiling brightly and proudly as she focusses attention on the newest member of their troupe.

As the audience shouted their praise and beat out their adulation and admiration with their clapping hands, Carlos could hardly contain the pride, joy, excitement and delight of this moment. From his first sight of that supple young girl in that distant dusty Columbian city some seven years previously, he had been on a journey of redemption. Now, having tasted the adrenalin of performance and the reward of the applause, if there had ever been any doubt before, Carlos was now well and truly an addict.

The future seemed bright and from now on for Carlos things could only get better. From here on in the only way was up: up onto the dental wire and further up onto the spinning Roman Rings. However, before attaining those dizzying heights there were some more mundane obstacles to overcome and further skills to be learned.

As the year wore on and the Cuban Missile Crisis almost brought the human race to complete extinction Carlos was to learn the more subtle aspects of his art. How to join the family in the big parade which took place at the start of all circus performances when the 'stars' give the audience a glimpse of what is to come. How to accept the applause directed towards him, while parading alongside other family members and how to graciously deflect it from himself and pass it on to other members of the troupe, using wide, generous open-armed gestures to share the adulation and bestow it upon the rest of the family.

The opening parades were fun, and in some ways frivolous moments in the show, where everyone was nervous and anxious to get down to the more serious business of their actual performance, but also happy to work together and willing to titillate and whet the appetite of the eager crowd. Performers rubbed shoulders, teased each other and competed in childish and risible ways, the whole circus coming together to keep the audience on their toes. These marketing ploys were also utilised during the parades presented when the circus arrived in town for the first time, with lavish displays being undertaken to ensure that everyone in the town or city knew of their arrival and that the talk of their outlandish behaviour and seemingly trans-human feats was on every tongue. All these displays of the exotic, and the awestruck clapping reward that they produced, were like raw adrenalin to Carlos. Here, now, all his suffering, all his hardship, all his rejection and betrayals were but nothing in the life-sustaining joy of the crowd's applause.

After all performance enhancement highs, whether induced by adrenalin, created by physical activity, or whether achieved through imbibing drugs like alcohol, smoking cannabis or injecting heroin there is always the sobering after effect: the come-down, when one is left bereft and in a completely different state, the state we tend to call 'normality' or 'every-day life', where the world seems mundane, drab, and disappointing and the dullness of repetitive activity seems to numb one's brain, in contrast to the excitement and creative rush of those heightened moments seconds before. The normal response to this is the desire to repeat the activity or intake of the drug that caused the original mind-altering experience. Carlos was no exception and in his case the desire to repeat the activity of 'performance' in order to achieve the reward of the 'applause' was to motivate and drive him forward for the next twenty-seven years.

Clearly it would take time to build up his act and to develop and create his own individual approach to performance. He was sensible enough to do this slowly and carefully. Learning from the family and honing his performance in the relative comfort and security that their benevolent presence afforded. From that initial performance in 1962, Carlos went on to create his own unique role in the troupe and before too long had his own solo spot in the family's section of the larger circus show.

While on the ground his performance was known as a 'carpet act', and as part of his total performance he would go through the same sequence of bends and twists on each occasion. Sometimes he would balance and contort on the knees of his adopted siblings. Sometimes he would perform a series of twists, bends and stretches while being held aloft by his circus father. Eventually he was to climb graciously up a slim rope, bending and stretching as he rose eventually climbing twenty to twenty-five feet into the air to perform initially rudimentary bends and spins on the Roman Rings. Before too long these routines had become more elaborate, and consequently more dangerous, as he became more and more daring, and more and more demanding feats and exertions. Ultimately he was to perform high up in the air, way above the audience's straining heads, hanging only by his teeth, much to the horror, fright and excitement of the breath-gasping crowd, spinning, gyrating and bending into seemingly impossible positions.

As time went on Carlos began to evolve his own philosophy in relation to performance. He had learned that his total performance should not last longer than about five minutes. The main reason for this, apart from the sheer physically exhausting demands it put upon him, was that he did not want to have the audience straining their necks looking up at him for too long. During this time his aerial performance consisted of him bending, stretch and contorting and enacting a range and predetermined sequence of moves, each more elaborate and 'daring' than the one before. He was also becoming more and more flamboyant. The confidence given to him by that first performance and the rapturous applause that accompanied it, led him to expose more and more of his true self.

Carlos had known from a very early age that he was different; he often felt that, although he was physically a man, somehow he was a woman within. His skill and ability as a contortionist gave him the opportunity to manifest and explore that hidden aspect of himself.

Alongside the 'boy wonder', Robin, from the Batman team, another hero of Carlos was Liberace, the outrageous, flamboyant and totally closeted homosexual, piano player. Carlos began to model himself on Liberace. He wanted to be like him. In his childish naivety Carlos – with a large portion of truth - considered himself to be a beautiful person. He was very muscular, had very sexy legs, and a very pretty and disarming personality. Like Liberace, women doted on him, wanting to mother and adopt him, so wherever he could, he added more elaborate costumes and more and more camp gestures defining and expressing himself in a way that began to feel more and more natural to him.

From his travels with the circus family, and from his position of relative wealth and privilege, he had soon come to realise that the people of South American were a very poor people. Carlos determined at a very early age that he wanted to give these people something he had never had himself. He felt a duty to try and improve and give value to their life for the five minutes he was before them in the ring. He wanted to give them something 'other worldly', something exotic and uplifting. His performance already provided that but, by becoming more and more flamboyant, though his gestures and eventually his costumes, Carlos felt that he could give them even more; something which would take them out of themselves, even if only for the duration of those few short minutes that he was performing before them. He realised that, even though he had his own hardships and difficulties, his audience had much bigger problems and this was his way of helping. This was his gift back to them, in return for the applause which they so freely and abundantly gave to him.

From the humble beginnings of that first public show in Lima in 1962, Carlos - or more correctly 'Robin' Medina - went on to become one of the greatest and most well respected aerial and dental contortionists of his time.

Chapter 5

A GLIMPSE OF A PERFORMANCE:
ROBERO'S CIRCUS – SOUTH AFRICA, 1980

Carlos gave his last performance in 1989 and sadly all that remains of his live act from a lifetime of performance is a short, poor quality video taken in 1980 when he was working for Robero's Circus in Johannesburg. I have tried below to give some sense of his performance from that video and hope that this, along with the various photographs scattered throughout the book, although they cannot really do justice to it, can give some sense of how remarkable his aerial performances actually were.

It is a hot, sultry evening in Johannesburg, South Africa, the temperature having cooled to a mere 18 degrees Centigrade from the daytime high of 23. The year is 1980 and we find ourselves inside the heavy dark canvas of the big top, which is supported by the thick white wooden poles that seem to stretch up into the darkness forever. We are sitting in the heat of the evening nestled among the expectant audience and experiencing a sense of awe, wonder and anticipation. We shift and fidget on the strange uncomfortable wooden benches which rise up in a series of steeply raked steps from the ring. Our nose twitches and sniffs at the unfamiliar and unusual odours that fill our nostrils; the smell of fresh sawdust wafting up from the ring, the more distant smell of animals, grease paint, and human sweat. The odd noises too: the neigh and snort of horses, and the stamp of impatient hooves, the distant shout of a lone performer, a loud trumpet sound - was that an elephant?

As we sit, trying to contain our excitement, our eyes slowly become accustomed to the dark, and in the pre-show tension we realize that, unlike a theatre, we can look across and see other audience members sitting opposite us, some distance away on the other side of the ring. Suddenly we are startled to attention by the sound of a small band beginning to play. Two huge follow spots snap on, painting a perfect circle of light on the ring below, the dust dancing in their powerful beams as they begin to chase each other across the darkness, like two full moons in an otherworldly sky. The excitement mounts, lights flood the ring, the ringmaster runs on, whip in hand, bows to the applauding crowd, welcomes us in several languages and the parade begins. Horses ride wildly round the ring, acrobats leaping on and off their backs, lions, in cages, roar as they are drawn into the light and displayed to the, by now, ecstatic crowd. The music seems to become increasingly more exciting as more and more acts spill into the ring to tantalize us with their performance. Soon the world-famous Circus March, the "Entrance of the Gladiators" (written by the little know Czech composer Julius Fučík) strikes up, as the clowns fall, stagger, leap and cavort into the ring. The circus has begun.

After the interval when it seems we can take no more, and following the 'Golden Elflett, which the expensive, full colour programme informs us is 'the Man with the Dancing Muscles' the lights dim to blackness and slowly the strains of the theme music to 'Cabaret' can be heard.

Suddenly, lights come up on a figure, sporting white leotards and wearing a white top that sparkles with a thousand sequins. He strides confidently into the centre of the ring. The programme informs us that this is '*The Queen (?) (sic) of the Air – ROBIN MEDINA*'. As he parades before us we see his cloak fanned out behind him. It too is pure white and sequin-clad, catching the light, wrapping it round him before sending beams hurtling back out into the darkness as he walks. Even his eyebrows, coated in white make-up, seem to shine and sparkle too.

He tours the ring like a king, making wide expansive arm gestures, carefully and meticulously taking in the whole of the crowd, performing polite, quick, head-bows at every stop. Business like, he unclasps the cloak and hands it to the Ring Master who has suddenly appeared out of the shrouding darkness to collect it, and then disappears again, vanishing without a trace.

Robin, now approaches a strange looking contraption which hangs, apparently unsupported about head-height from the floor. It appears to be a silver metal bar, like a trapeze, but with large metal rings and ropes hanging from it. As he reaches it we suddenly notice that he has been carrying something in his left hand all this time. He now attaches this strange object to a hook in the centre of the bar and places the other end in his mouth. The band does not skip a beat as Robin holding on to the bar, but with his teeth firmly grasping the mouth-piece, slowly begins to rise into the air. As the bar rises higher and higher into the darkness he takes his hands off the bar, and goes through a series of graceful and expressive motions with them. It's only then that it fully dawns upon us that he is doing all this while hanging on solely by his teeth.

The Cabaret theme ends and the music suddenly changes, turning from the extravagant upbeat cabaret sound into the slow haunting theme from

Tchaikovsky's Swan Lake - 'The Dance of the Dying Swan'. Robin, still ascending begins to contort before us, gracefully stretching his arms and his legs. Watching in silent awe we realize that he has taken hold of both ankles and has drawn his legs up behind his back and is now hanging by his teeth, holding the position of a full back-bend. The white sparkling costume, the dirge-like music, and the effortlessly smooth streamlined sequence of contortions, make us realize we are watching an aerial ballet: a re-interpretation of Swan Lake some thirty or so feet up in the air.

With a quick tug on the ropes he releases two large rings and they drop his body length below him. Carefully putting a foot in each ring, and allowing them to take his weight he slowly stretches his legs wider and wider apart, finally executing a perfect full body length version of the splits. From here, he gracefully lifts and places his left knee into the left ring while, placing his right knee in the right ring, unbelievably he is now hanging upside down supported only by his knees. He moves again and in shock we realize that he is supporting his full weight on just one knee. Not content with that, he moves again adopting a full back bend, his right leg being held over his right shoulder. The audience applauds loudly at each and all of the various turns, twist and changes of position. All these moves appear to be so simple to execute and are simultaneously made to look graceful, effortless and presented with a full happy smile so that we are completely taken by the skill of it all, forgetting the level of discipline and flexibility involved, and the muscular demands that such a routine must be making on his body.

As he continues his routine the music approaches its haunting climax and with his right knee in the right hand-ring and supporting his body weight in the left-hand ring by only his left ankle, he slowly bends forwards, arm outstretched, looking for all the world like the pale white remnants of the dying swan. As he lies motionless for what seem to be several timeless moments, holding that strenuous recumbent pose, it dawns on us that it can be seen as a tribute not only to the dying swan of Petipa and Ivanov's ballet, but also, perhaps, a fitting tribute to the little lithe figure of the young girl who, so many, many, years before, was the initial inspiration for this, his crowning achievement.

The pose complete, we are snapped out of Swan Lake and into a jazzy up-tempo beat as Robin begins to rotate at greater and greater speed. The motion is at once terrifying and fascinating for he begins to spin faster and faster. It is mesmeric. His limbs seem to fly into unusual positions, legs appear over his shoulders, he twists and turns rotating through space, transforming effortlessly, only to pause briefly having adopted yet another mind-challenging position. As the music increases in volume and tempo we find it hard to believe our eyes. With his left knee in one ring and holding the other ring in his right hand, his right leg bent up and being held onto the back of his head, he begins to spin again. His whole body is gyrating in space, faster and faster, until he is almost a white blur against the blackness of the thick dark canvas high above him. The final chords chime together, crashing and banging to their crescendo as the spinning figure eventually slows and then stops, grabs the rings with his hands, and is slowly and majestically lowered to the ground. It's over. The audience break into involuntary and rapturous applause. He is now on the ground standing before us mouthing 'thank-you' and acknowledging our obvious delight. Then after a series of short sharp bows, he takes one final bow and skips gaily out of the ring. Although the whole routine has taken only five minutes, it seems like a lifetime.

Chapter 6

ROBIN MEDINA – AERIAL
CONTORTIONIST

The circus family continued to tour the length and breadth of South America, sometimes even venturing over to the Caribbean. In 1972 Carlos and the family were in Ecuador performing with the *"Circo Egred de Colombia"*.

The following year they visited Bolivia, Paraguay, Panama, Bogotá and Argentina. With the constant travel, the demands of daily performance, and the rigorous training that supports it, it is hardly surprising that over time, with the lack of any real blood-ties to bind them together, the strains of circus life began to create tensions within the 'family' unit. Also as the children matured and grew more independent, and more assertive, keeping the family together was becoming more of a challenge. Meneco, as we have already seen, had been up and gone some time before, being, in Carlos' opinion, much braver and more independent than Carlos ever was. Sonia had eventually come to the conclusion that she was a lesbian, and wanted to be free to explore that side of herself, although she did remain performing with the family. Marlene fell in love, eventually got pregnant, and had a baby called Sandra, and after some turbulent scenes she too remained in the fold. Carlos himself was to remain and perform as part of the 'family' troupe until July 1974, when he was twenty-four years old.

When the time came for Carlos to finally leave the 'Circus family' that he had been sold into as a child, he was a mature and seasoned performer. He was known and respected throughout the Circus world. His performances created a mixture of fear and admiration in his audiences, and he had been fawned and fêted by the rich and famous. So, when rumours of his potential departure began to circulate in the Circus community, it is really no surprise to learn that Carlos was approached by many who were eager to provide him with work in the next phase of his career.

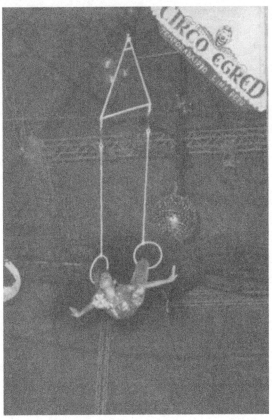

Carlos at the age of 20 hanging by his knees from the Roman Rings, in Lima with Circo Egred in 1972

Carlos and *Truppe Algecidas* were performing once again in Lima when Carlos first began to declare openly that he was intending to leave the troupe and become a solo artist. The word spread quickly, and within a few days of his beginning to talk openly about this potential new future he was approached by Señor Atayde, the Circus Director of the Atayde Brothers Circus (*Circo Hermanos Atayde*)

Señor Atayde was clearly very aware of Carlos and *Las Truppe Algeciras*, although the 'circus family' never had any professional dealings with Circus Atayde. Regardless of this, Mr Atadye was a very friendly and generous man, and at this particular meeting extended to Carlos an opened-ended opportunity, offering to provide Carlos with a season of work whenever he wanted it. In a moment of triumph and as if to assert his independence Carlos quickly accepted this kind offer, and in July 1974, when the family contract had finished in Peru, Carlos flew alone to Mexico City to begin his first season working for Mr Atayde and the *Circo Hermanos Atayde*.

A circus season can vary greatly. With some circuses the season can be six months long, with others only three months. Indeed with some, a season can be as short as four nights. Factors that affect the duration of a season range from the size of the town, and therefore the size of the audience, to things like the weather. The climate too can have a huge impact upon whether the show can go on or not. Sometimes, depending on the country, tropical storms and hurricanes can make it impossible for the crew to raise the big top. Sometimes, the winter can be so heavy that the circus is unable to travel. And sometimes they can just get stuck en-route and never reach their destination. All these factors come into play when the circus begins to tour, and possibly explains the high level of superstition among circus folk.

In many ways Carlos was making a huge leap of faith. Not only was he putting his trust in the word of Mr Atayde, but he was also gambling his future career. For, once having burnt his bridges with *Las Truppe Algeciras,* there may have been no one to go back to. So, here at the tender age of twenty-four, as part of his first freelance undertaking, we find Carlos on a plane flying to take up his first engagement, with no real assurances that it was going to happen. His faith, trust and confidence in Mr Atadye however, proved justified and his initial contract ended up being for a four-and-a-half month long season, travelling with the most prestigious circus in Mexico. As it happened, the mutual friendship and trust between the two men was so strong and their confidence and faith in each other so sure, that Carlos actually ending up staying with Mr Atayde well beyond that first season.

The *Circo Hermanos Atayde* - Atayde Brothers Circus - was a very old family circus based in Mexico, founded by Aurelio Atayde Guizar and his brothers in Zacatecas on August 26, 1888. The story goes that the founder, Aurelio Atayde Guízar, actually ran away from home as a child to join a circus. Later, Aurelio convinced his other brothers to come and join him and found their own company. Although based in Mexico City, the circus toured widely through Central and South America. For publicity and promotional purposes each major circus adopts its own colour scheme and the Atayde family was no exception, choosing to use a bright orange and grey livery; colours which very quickly became familiar and popular with the peoples of Mexico, as the circus toured from town to town.

When Carlos joined *Circo Hermanos Atayde* in 1974, Mexico had a population of around 62 million people, so there was seldom any real need to for the Circus to venture outside the country to find an audience.

At that time Mexico City - their home base - had a population of well over eight and half million people and so one could argue they had little need to even tour out of that city at all. However, as the nature of the circus gene seems to be, touring was very much a part of their intrinsic DNA.

Having secured his first solo engagement so swiftly, and with such a prestigious host, one would have been forgiven for thinking that all should have been plain sailing for Carlos from now on. However, as if unwilling to let him go and, possibly, as a result of being away from their protective penumbra, it seemed the teeth of the menacing 'circus family' clown could still bite. Shortly after joining the Atayde Brother, Carlos had his first serious fall. This happened while he was performing in the Mexican city of *Oaxaca* some 300 miles south of Mexico City. One day during training Carlos twisted his ankle, and although he could still walk, it meant he was out of action for three or four weeks. This was a major blow to him. Here he was, a young man striking out in the world suddenly - almost literally - stopped in his tracks.

It would, of course, take more than a simple fall to stop Carlos but this accident did afford him the opportunity to explore the city of *Oaxaca*. While there he visited and was greatly impressed by a very famous tree known as El *Árbol del Tule* (Spanish for The *Tree of Tule*). The tree, a Montezuma cypress, is considered to be the second stoutest tree in the world, with a diameter of 11.42 metres, and it is thought to be about one thousand four hundred years old. It is also said that it takes about twenty-five people holding hands together, to wrap around it. Carlos was greatly struck by the enormity of this tree, and the image of all those people holding hands to embrace it stuck firmly in his imagination.

After the slight mishap of his fall, Carlos was soon up and performing again and as their time together went on Mr Atayde came to respect Carlos more and more as a professional and polished performer. The two men soon built up a strong and deep emotional friendship. Mr Atayde and his whole family seemed very keen to do all he and they could to help Carlos further his career.

Throughout the remainder of 1974 *Circo Hermanos Atayde* continued to tour through the major towns and cities of Mexico. While they were performing in Monterrey, a city located in the north east of Mexico about a hundred miles from the border with the USA, Mr Atayde was approached by an old friend, a certain Señor Gasca, who had a favour to ask.

Señor Alexander Fuentes Gasca, Director of *Circo Hermanos Fuentes Gasca*, was a very wealthy and powerful man and owned with his family - circuses tend to favour nepotism - a total of three separate circuses. One of these was called *Circo de Mexico Juventino Fuentes Gasca* and tended to be based in and around Mexico, while another called *Circo Norte Americano* tended to travel further afield, and it is the latter circus that we are interested in. Additionally, Señor Fuentes it seemed, when not managing his three circuses, was a very virile man and over the years had expanded and secured his family dynasty by producing some twenty five children from five different wives!

It soon transpired that his reason for approaching Mr Atayde on this occasion was to discover if Mr Atayde thought Carlos would want to come and work for him. He explained to Mr Atayde that he had seen Carlos perform with his family, *Las Truppe Algeciras* in Peru, in Bolivia and also in Panama and was very keen to engage him. He also knew about the changes that had recently taken place in Carlos' former 'Circus Family' and how Marlene had fallen in love and had left to have her baby. Mr Atayde was, of course, very keen to help and said he would approach Carlos and explain to him that the renowned, Señor Fuentes, was interested in him joining his circus, *Circo Norte Americano*.

Unsurprisingly Mr Atayde lost no time in informing Carlos that the Fuentes family were interested in having him work for them in their forthcoming season, and additionally explained that they were keen for him to perform high up in the big top on the opposite side of the tent to the 'famous aeroplane'.

Now the so called 'famous aeroplane', was well known in circus lore, having been built in the nineteen-forties for a very great American lady aerialist called Celeste. Celeste was reputedly a very beautiful and glamorous woman, and Celeste's husband was a Russian émigré who had fled from Russia during the thirties and become a naturalised American. He also appears to have been a very skilled fabricator, and it was he who built the winged device for his wife, after she dreamt up the seemingly crazy idea of flying in an aeroplane inside the big top. The contraption not only looked like an aeroplane, it actually had two engines the propellers of which spun round, simulating actual flight. When it first appeared this was a startling idea and the crowds, many of whom would never have seen a real aeroplane let alone a model, could only gasp in wonder and amazement unable to work out how the beautiful Celeste was able to fly such a complex machine in such a confined space. It was a great success and Celeste and her aeroplane were a major crowd-pulling attraction for many years.

Carlos (now aged 24) suspended by his teeth and literally 'flying' through the air, balanced by a mock-up aeroplane made for 'Celeste'. The picture was taken in Mexico while Carlos was touring with Circo Norte Americano.

When she retired the Fuentes family approached Celeste to ask if she wanted to sell the rig for the aeroplane. Clearly having no further need for it herself she quickly agreed. It was then very promptly installed high up in the big top and became a regular feature of the Circo Norte Americano. So, it was to be here, adjacent to this very famous crowd magnet of an aeroplane, that Señor Fuentes wanted Carlos to perform. But not only that, the wily circus owner wanted to make Carlos a star, and had devised a whole act that he thought would complement Carlos' aerial vivacity.

The act which Señor Fuentes had dreamt up, possibly based on that of the glamorous act Celeste had performed, was that Carlos would appear as an impressive Scandinavian Prince, with long flowing blonde hair, and a costume reminiscent of the Viking Valkyrie attire of Brünnhilde, from Wagner's *Ring*.

Flamboyant, vivacious, outrageous and extravagant though Carlos was, even he was left speechless for several seconds by this crazy notion. After he regained his composure Carlos shrugged, thought to himself, 'nothing ventured nothing gained' and agreed. Eventually, in the process of a later negotiation, Carlos was able to insist on a simplified costume. He also made clear his demands that he did not want to appear with cheap bleached blond hair but wanted to be a platinum blond like Marilyn Monroe. Having got most of his way the eager Señor Fuentes readily agreed to all these demands and the deal was done.

They say an artist often has to suffer for his art and Carlos was no exception. Nowadays our streets are full of people who have dyed their hair a new and vibrant colour. Normally they have been able to do this in the comfort of their own homes, and often, the colour they have chosen has not just been blonde, but one taken from a whole rainbow-coloured pallet of other shades, tones and tints. Unfortunately for Carlos, forty years ago, when he decided to go blonde for his art, the process required to enable him to dye his hair took nine-and-a-half hours! Not only that, but so healthy was the natural growth rate of his hair that after six or seven days the black roots began to show through again, and he had to repeat the whole process from the beginning. Regardless of these initial sacrifices the act proved to be a great success and was another very successful step on the ladder to stardom for Carlos' rapidly growing Circus reputation.

Carlos continued to tour and perform for the great Señor Fuentes and his family, up and down the length and breadth of continental South America. He also soon dropped the time-consuming platinum blonde mane, for his more natural flowing black hair. Carlos had become the successful solo star of his dreams. Here he was, performing at the peak of his physical ability, in one of the most famous circuses in South America thrilling and amazing the ever delighted and marvelling crowds far below, and for himself drinking up their gratitude and applause like a hungry baby sucking down his mother's milk. Time went by. As Carlos circled the ring at the end of his act performing his bows and thanking the crowd, it was as if he had become like the hands of a clock - with every turn of the ring he was changing the minutes into hours, the hours into days, the days into weeks, the weeks into months, and the months into years.

Sometime during 1977 another famous face appeared on the scene, keen to talk seriously with Señor Fuentes. This face belonged to a certain Raul Prada. Originally from Columbia, Raul Prada had had a very successful international career as a high-wire artist but after a crippling fall he was destined to spend the rest of his life in a wheelchair. This had not deterred him in any way and he very quickly adapted to his new situation, and had subsequently gone on to become a very famous and well respected Circus Agent. He was especially known for hiring acts for circuses which toured in the USA. Unlike Señor Fuentes, Raul Prada had no crazy schemes to make Carlos into some lavish North American Indian princess, but rather, was in a bit of a jam. He had previously booked an act to appear in Las Vegas for a short season, but the artist in question had been touring in Europe and had, for one reason or another, been delayed in returning and so would be unable to fulfil the Las Vegas contract. Rather than cancel the engagement, Raul Prada had come to see if Carlos would step into the breach. Of course, when he learned of this opportunity Carlos was delighted to help and Señor Fuentes was magnanimous about letting him go. So, for three to four weeks in mid-1977 Carlos thrilled the crowds in Las Vegas gambling with his life as he spun and gyrated high above them, while they continued to gambled away their lives and their money on the tables and fruit machines far below.

Shortly before his trip to Las Vegas, Carlos, or rather Señor Fuentes, had been approached by yet another and probably more famous Circus Director, Mr Hubert Castle owner and director of the *Hubert Castle International Shrine Circus.* A deal had very quickly been struck and Carlos was scheduled to join Hubert Castle for the start of the 1978 season.

The contract to perform with Herbert Castle was supposed to be a secret, but while he was in Las Vegas, Raul Prada, began to express a great deal of concern to Carlos about the prospect of him going to work for Hubert Castle. Carlos was very surprised and wanted to know how Raul had heard about this contract. It transpired that two of Señor Fuentes many sons, in this case Gustava and Rodin, had spilled the beans to Raul, as they too had concerns about Mr Castle. So much for keeping it in the family!

Raul Prada pressed on with his concern telling Carlos that Hubert Castle was very racist, and not only that, he was also extremely anti-gay, adding, as if to substantiate his claim, "He's from Texas."

Not one to be scared off by controversy or prejudice Carlos was rather exasperated and boldly told Raul Prada. "Raul, he wants me for my act. Not for my body! He doesn't want to know about my private life! Surely I won't be the first gay man who has ever gone to work for Hubert Castle?"

Silenced by this verbal rebuke, Raul decided to pursue the matter no further, and it was possibly just as well. Reflecting back on his time working for Hubert Castle, Carlos recalls that Mr Hubert Castle was always a perfect gentlemen to him, in fact, "...a lovely, lovely, gentleman."

Chapter 7

DYSFUNCTIONAL FAMILIES

Despite the best efforts of the Christian Church, the philosophy espoused by the citizens and Presidents of the USA and fully endorsed by that land of myth and magic known as Hollywood, along with the pronouncements and sentiments expressed by various other forms of Governments and religious practitioners around the world, the notion of the loving caring family does seem to be something of a myth. We only need to look at some recent news headlines to see a different reality. If we go back even further to Biblical times we may recall the story of Abraham, so quick and so willing to sacrifice his only son Isaac at the bidding of his God, along with endless tales of other troublesome families from that era. We may also recall from our readings in history and literature, all that trouble in Greece with Laius and his son Oedipus. Then, comparatively recently, we may recall in Shakespeare's day we have his account of that whole awkward issue with Hamlet and the Danish court. Clearly families are not easy, and father and son relationships in particular can be extremely difficult emotional terrain to manoeuvre and navigate through, sometimes even seemingly downright impossible.

Carlos was no exception in this regard either, having found it almost impossible to even consider approaching his own father, never mind following in his footsteps. When we look back at his early life and learn of his problems with his real father, or rather his real father's problem with him, in that he did not want him, his subsequent abuse by his church 'father' and the disinterest, distain and exploitation by his 'circus father', it should come as no surprise to us, that to Carlos, the notion of the 'happy, loving family' and the supposition that there will be 'the formation of a strong bond between a father and his son', is viewed with some scepticism.

Having left his real family in 1959 Carlos probably assumed that he would never see them again. However, towards the end of 1977 events were to take a turn that would propel him back, if not into their arms, at least into their proximity.

As we learned while he was in Las Vegas the fact that Carlos was about to join Hubert Castle's Circus was not a closely guarded secret. Carlos joined the Hubert Castle International Shrine Circus toward the end of the 1977 season. He had been engaged to be the star of the show for 1978, and appeared with them once or twice as they were winding down towards the Christmas holidays to get accustomed to the staff, the other performers and the general running order, and operation of the show. Of course, his name would not appear in the 1977 programme, which would have been printed long before, but he would be expected to use the few remaining weeks of the tour to settle in to what was to be his new home and new family for the forthcoming season.

The *Hubert Castle International Shrine Circus* was different to most circuses that Carlos had worked with so far in that instead of performing under a big top, they tended to perform in permanent venues; conference centres, civic auditoriums and sports arenas and sometimes even outdoors in the open air. Because of this they were able to tour much more rapidly, having less equipment to transport. To facilitate this rapid method of touring,

Carlos had been given his own motor home and his own driver.

Carlos caught up with the show while they were in Kansas City in early November 1977. The show itself was running down to its end of season and winter break and was experiencing some problems. On the second of November two members of the *'Rodriquez Troupe'* who were aerial artists, were injured when they fell. Apparently, they were about to climb up into the rigging to perform their act when the security net they were standing on suddenly collapsed. Clearly this was not an auspicious start to Carlos' involvement with the Hubert Castle Circus as he too was an aerial artist, but then again it could have been more to do with Kansas City.

Kansas City, in the state of Missouri, was famous for being a rough, dangerous, and violent place as far back as the American Civil War. Missouri was on the border between the Confederate states to the south and east and the northern states to the north and west, which resulted in Kansas City being divided into two distinct pro-slavery and anti-slavery camps. After the war the local paper the *Kansas City Times* helped turn outlaw and gang leader Jesse James into a folk hero. In the twentieth century, the infamous Democratic Party "Boss" Tom Prendergast, through his corruption and the flouting of prohibition helped the Kansas City become the country's "most wide-open town". This in turn led to the arrival of organised crime in the shape of the mafia 'mob' along with a huge influx of desperate immigrants. During the time Carlos was there, in the late 1970's, mob violence in the shape of gangland slayings or 'hits' still took place from time to time. The streets were also full of poor starving immigrants who had come to America chasing the America Dream but ended up living on the streets in homeless squalor and existing, hand to mouth.

Whether Carlos was aware of the violence seething just under the surface of the city and sometimes bursting openly on to its streets, or whether he was more concerned with containing the troubling violent emotions towards his father which rose within him from time to time, engendering feelings of rage, rejection and loneliness, we are unsure, but both these separate and real, rivers of violence, were about to converge into a mighty ocean of storm lashed pain.

The Hubert Castle's Circus was performing inside a large Convention Centre type building in the centre of the city and, due to the urban nature of the venue, it was clearly not possible for the performers to adhere to the usual arrangements of parking their caravans and mobile homes close to, or even inside the safety afforded by the venue. Carlos found himself and his driver having to park some mile and a half away from the circus proper.

After taking his bows from the final performance of the evening, and waving to the appreciative crowd, Carlos, as he was leaving the ring, was approached by the rather agitated looking Ringmaster the so called 'Colonel Lucky Larabee'. The Colonel's normal military-like demeanour was seriously dented, and he looked very troubled and deeply concerned about something. As Carlos approached him, he could hold back his concern no longer and blurted out, "Mr Medina, they have broken into your caravan. Do you have any insurance?" After a moment's shock to take in the import of the question, Carlos was able to assure him that he had insurance, and they both set off at great speed to examine the damage.

The Motor Home that Carlos was living in was not well fortified, not having been designed for such eventualities. When they reached it, both Carlos and the Colonel could clearly see that the door had been violently broken open, and was almost snapped off its hinges. Inside a mirror had been smashed and all Carlos' possessions and papers were strewn across the interior as if it had been hit by a tornado. The concerned Colonel insisted that Carlos check to see if all his crucial papers were there. After searching for some time through the detritus of his normally neat and tidy home, Carlos concluded that his passport had been stolen. This was very bad news indeed. Due to the strict immigration policy of the United States, Colonel Larabee informed Carlos that he had only seventy-eight hours in which to leave the country. He would then be required to get all his papers in order and obtain a new visa before he was able to return. Lucky Larabee kindly agreed to sign a declaration for Carlos explaining what had happened, and assured Carlos that this declaration would assist Carlos in obtaining the correct paper work in order to process his visa.

As the enormity of the situation began to dawn upon both men, it became apparent that Carlos would require a new passport, and that the only person who could vouch for him was his father, in far off Cúcuta, Columbia. Armed with the declaration letter from the generous Colonel, Carlos set off on an unanticipated and unwelcome journey from Kansas City to Minneapolis then to Florida and finally on to Bogota in order to return to his familial home, some twenty years after having been cast out from it.

This return journey must have been as painful and traumatic as that first bus journey away from his home, travelling with his new and as yet unknown 'circus family' when the smart of rejection had lacerated his tiny boyish heart and crippled his emotions with its callous cruelty. Having had to deal with all the anger and rage that he felt as a nine-year old boy when his father so cruelly and calculatingly had sold him into the circus, Carlos was unsure how he would feel or react when he met him again. He was nervous, anxious and agitated, and the long halting journey, with its many changes, would have done nothing to alleviate his uncertainty and fear. By now his two allies, Lola, his grandmother and, Eloise, his great-grandmother were both long dead, and his father was an old man of sixty three or sixty four years of age.

Strangely enough, when he finally confronted his father after all that time, in the dusty darkness of his former home, Carlos was very surprised to discover that someone who had had such an emotionally devastating impact on his life could look so small and insignificant. The overwhelming response that Carlos had to the meeting was that there was nothing special about him. This man, this being, who had raged through Carlos' mind as an horrific and gigantic monster, hell-bent on destroying him, now looked like a pathetic, selfish little child with odd, sad, cross, squinting eyes. To the strong, fit, healthy young Carlos who was now a renowned circus star in his own right, this mean, bitter, twisted looking little shell of an old man could only inspire pity.

Very little in the way of words transpired between them during his stay. His father was cold, distant and dismissive and seemed to be simmering just below the surface with a thinly disguised hostility. It was far too late for any recriminations on Carlos' part, and the making of any act of contrition and begging for forgiveness never seemed to have entered his father's consideration. One day however, when his father seemed to be in a lighter mood, Carlos attempted to find out a little bit more about the one completely unknown person in his life - his mother. Although she had abandoned him and had never attempted to contact him since and although Carlos had determined never to search for her, it was natural that he should still be curious about such a crucial figure: as the woman who had brought him into this world. The answer his father returned to him was so vicious, so painful and so hurtful that even today just trying to recall that response can reduce Carlos to tears. The remainder of his time there was to be tainted by the dark and deadly shadow of these cutting remarks and Carlos was eager to be off.

Despite his cold reception and the cruel and contemptuous way his father spoke of his mother, Carlos was still able to be magnanimous. He was no longer a child, and was able to relate to this shrivelled, bitter little creature in a mature and sympathetic way and with an adult perspective. *The world is suffering.* Through his various travels and encounters with so many people and so many different cultures, Carlos had seen and experienced first-hand the hardship, pain and suffering that life can inflict. Now older and wiser he was in a position to 'understand', but never forgive, his father's reasons for jumping at the opportunity that the circus had presented and for wanting to rid himself of an extra, hungry young mouth, and of an enduring responsibility.

After his father's vitriolic response to his questions about his mother Carlos determined to focus on his reason for being there and quickly went about the perfunctory task of ensuring his father signed the various papers and all the authorisations that he required in order to obtain a new passport. Having concluded his business, he then left the hot, dusty, cattle-smelling hell-hole of a home as promptly as possible and set off north. He caught a plane from Bogota to Miami and then on to Chicago and, with his new passport in hand and Lucky Larabee's letter of endorsement, was swiftly able to obtain a new visa to remain and perform in the USA. The power of the Shriners' endorsement opened doors that often required long hours and sometimes weeks and months of patient waiting. As the already engaged potential 'star' of their 1978 season, Carlos was warmly and enthusiastically welcomed back into the *Hubert Castle International Shrine Circus* with open arms.

Carlos was never to see his father alive again. When his father eventually died in 1987 Carlos did make the journey back to Columbia to attend the funeral, but the reception was incredibly hostile and unpleasant. His father's brother (Carlos' uncle) tried to stop him attending the event. He told Carlos that he was not welcome there, and that they did not want 'queers' hanging around. At one point he even apparently threatened to kill Carlos if he ever turned up there again. Having been so warmly and generously welcomed into the bosom of his extended family it is hardly surprising that Carlos never ventured back to Cúcuta again.

Chapter 8

SOLO ARTIST - LIFE ON THE ROAD

The Shrine Circuses are a largely philanthropic organization and have been dubbed the "World's Greatest Philanthropy." The Shrine fraternity, is part of the Family of Freemasons, and the ease with which Carlos obtained his visa to re-enter the USA, is testament to the power and influence of this historic organization. It is recorded that *the Ancient Arabic Order of the Nobles of the Mystic Shrine* (A.A.O.N.M.S.) was founded in 1872 in New York, by Walter Fleming and since 2010 have been known as Shriners International.

Walter Fleming had gathered together a group of thirteen fellow Master Masons for the sole purpose of creating his new organisation. It seems the thinking behind the Shiners was that that the Masons needed something less serious in their rituals and Fleming was keen to provide them with the opportunity to come together with less emphasis on ritual and more emphasis on fun, including even a light libation from time to time. Apparently, it was Fleming who drafted the Shriners ritual, designed the emblem and costumes, formulated a salutation and declared that members would wear a red fez. The idea of having more fun seems to have been a sound one and was very quickly adopted by other Masons; before long new Shrine lodges sprang up in fairly rapid succession across the USA

The Shrine fraternity's objective is three-fold: to participate in good fun and fellowship, develop lasting friendships and to take an active role in providing relief for those in need. In 1922, the Shrine fraternity decided to support the needs of children suffering from certain birth defects, diseases, burns and orthopaedic medical problems without the children, or their families, incurring any cost whatsoever. This they would do regardless of race, religion, or their relationship to a Shriner. To achieve this, they set up a network of twenty-two specialist Shrine Hospitals. There are now approximately 191 Shrine chapters in the United States, Canada, Mexico, and Panama and the Shrine Circuses engage annual international tours to raise money for the group's charity.

Of course, even though the Shriners' were all about philanthropy, a circus performer cannot live by bread alone. The Shrine Circuses were run on a sound commercial basis and Carlos received a wage for his efforts, but every so often special performances would be set aside dedicated to fund-raising for specific Shriner causes. Throughout 1978 we find Carlos touring with Hubert Castle's Shrine Circus and visiting a whole serious of Shrine Circuses as part of a non-stop and at times seemingly breath-taking tour.

Until his engagement with Hubert Castle in the USA we have had to rely solely upon Carlos for the details of his circus life, for it appears, that records of South American tours and circuses are much less well documented than those in the North. A great bonus for anyone researching circuses in the USA is *Circus Report*, an America weekly which was first published in 1972 and ran reviews, short news stories, adverts and obituaries. It covered most of the major activity in the American circuses for that week, including listing where those circuses were due to perform, what routes they would follow, and details about which artists were scheduled to perform. Contributions to the magazine came from a variety of reporters, some of whom were circus owners, performers and sometimes just fans.

With the help of *Circus Report* we know that Carlos first appeared in the programme for Hubert Castle in the 1978 season which opened on 14th Jan in Flint Michigan and ran there until the 22nd January. On January the 23rd they moved on to Grand Rapids, Michigan and played there until the 29th.

On February the 18th, the Circus appeared in Mentor, Ohio, playing there for just three nights until 20th. From February 25th until March 5th we find the Circus appeared at the Zuhrah Shrine Circus in Minneapolis, Minnesota. On March 10th, the circus pops up in Boseman, Montana, and by March 22 we find Carlos is spinning high up at the Al Kader Shrine Circus, in the Memorial Coliseum, Portland, Oregon until the 25th.

In April - from the 13th-16th - the Hubert Castle Circus found itself in Indianapolis, Indiana. While in May from the 8th to the 11th they have suddenly arrived in Regina, Saskatchewan, Canada. Later that month they moved on to Calgary.

Clearly for a circus touring was all! During the first five months of 1978 Carlos and the Circus covered a distance of well over 4,519 miles (7273 kilometres) - further than the distance between London and New York - and it was only just May! The sheer logistics of organising such a whirlwind tour are staggering.

However, as we have already noted, Hubert Castle Circus did not have the encumbrance of a Big Top to haul round with them. They had adopted the more common practice of the time playing in existing venues: other shrine circuses, conference centres and even sports arenas. This made the seemingly incomprehensible distances they travelled more understandable.

Because he did not drive Hubert Castle had arranged for Carlos to have use of a motor home, along with his own driver a certain Una Alber. Mr Alber was a rather rough and ready Cuban trapeze artist, who seems to have had some minor role in the main show. When telling me about him and their travels together Carlos did a wonderful impersonation of him. He spoke in really broken Spanish, which Carlos found difficult to follow, not always understanding what he was saying, Cuban Spanish being pronounced differently from mainland Spanish, more like a very strong regional accent. Mr Alber often used to lecture Carlos on the need for him to learn to drive, pointing out that Carlos could not expect to live in hotels all his life. At that time Carlos found the idea of driving far too butch and masculine for his tastes. Mr Alber insisted that driving was easy, you just needed one hand on the wheel and the other under your bottom. We should bear in mind that the majority of American Cars are automatics and given the vast distances they were covering this probably was the most comfortable position to adopt for a two or three-hour long drive.

The rest of the year reads just as breathlessly. In June the Circus hurtled up into the West Coast of Canada with the following head-spinning dates: June 5 Grand Prairie, Alberta, June 6th Dawson Creek, British Columbia, June 7-8 Prince George, 9th Williams Lake, 10th Kamloops, and on the 11th Revelstoke. On 12th June we find them in Vernon, British Columbia, 13th in Kelowna, 14th in Penticton, 15th Chilliwack, and 16-18th in Vancouver.

A brief note in Circus Report for Sept 25th 1978 indicates that "*More shows favoured Western Canada in 1978 than in any previous year to date.*" It appears that through late July and August Hubert Castle's show was in competition with other Canadian and international shows for audiences. During September (8th to 12th) the Hubert Castle Circus was playing to audiences that filled the grandstand and track at the Western Fair, in London, Ontario. Possibly as a result of the aforementioned level of competition, Castle and his ringmaster Col. Lucky Larraby (the spelling of whose name seems to vary enormously) changed the format of the show. Rather than the usual two-hour performance in the evening, they introduced the idea of doing a one-hour performance; three times a day; thus, enabling Castle to split up his troupe to deliver three different shows.

By October (4th-8th) they have left Canada far behind and we find the Hubert Castle Circus back in the USA but way down south at El Paso, Texas sponsored by the Alhambra Shrine. Then in a very odd shift of direction in early November we find them on the other side of the country, high up on the east coast in Utica, New York State, where the show featured Robin Medina performing for the Ziyara Shrine Temple.

For the remaining seven months of the year they managed to clock up a staggering 8000 miles. However, with all this constant travel and performance Carlos was about to have a short busman's holiday.

Early in 1978, while Carlos was touring with Hubert Castle in Indianapolis, the Vice President of Entertainment Programming for Toronto based Canadian Television Company (CTV), Arthur Weinthal, came up with the novel idea of doing a Television series about the circus. The pilot episode of the show, entitled simply, *Circus*, was broadcast on April 16th 1978. The original pilot show was an hour long, and reputedly featured Canadian Comedian, Leslie Nielsen (famous for 'Naked Gun' and 'Airplane' films) as the ringmaster. Unfortunately, I can find no credit for this show in Nielsen's biography, so perhaps he just did not want to be remembered for it. Certainly he never seems to have appeared in the show again.

The format for the show was a very odd mix indeed. Songs were performed by Cal Dodd and Sherisse Laurence two young starry-eyed hopefuls, who went on to become the regular co-hosts of the show, and thereby made their careers. Meanwhile, in between songs, live performances by known circus acts, were interspersed.

Despite, or because of, it's strange marrying of various performing arts, the show was a great success. After the initial pilot episode, the shows were reduced to half-an-hour in duration, and a first season, consisting of 24 episodes was commissioned, with the first show being broadcast on September 22nd 1978. The show was very well received and *Circus* very quickly went on to become the darling of Canadian TV, being referred to as *'Canada's number one Canadian Entertainment Program'*. After the first season was complete the show went back to being an hour long and continued to run until 1985.

Possibly as a result of being in the right place at the right time Carlos was invited to appear on the show, and featured in Episode 23 of the first season, which was broadcast on March 9th 1979. The show was taped in advance and *Circus Report* notes, in their October 2nd 1978 edition, that, "*Robin Medina, iron jaw*" was one of several acts that were being recorded for the show. The term 'Iron Jaw' is actually circus slang, usually used by the riggers and navy's who set up the Big Top. It refers - accurately enough - to: "An aerial act in which an acrobat swings and does tricks while hanging from a suspended mouth piece."

The recordings for the first season took place in the CTV studios in Toronto from August 28 through to Sept 8, which coincides with the time Carlos was performing with Hubert Castle in London, Ontario, just over an hour's drive away.

The blurb that came out from CTV about Episode 23 unfortunately not only bills him alongside a boxing kangaroo and a perch act but also managed to spell Carlos' name wrong and reads:-

Mar 9, 1979 - Cal Dodd and Sherisse Laurence welcome Boomer the Boxing Kangaroo, the Aguilas perch act, the Claytons' wire act and Robin Madina's (sic) iron jaw act. Hosts Cal Dodd and Sherisse Laurence sing "Soolaimon."

As well as the co-hosts singing the Neil Diamond song "Soolaimon", Carlos seems to recall Cal and Sherisse singing the Elton John/Kiki Dee hit, "Don't Go Breaking My Heart", while he was going through his heart-racing routine high above the studio floor.

As we have mentioned the circus translates into many languages because it is visual and therefore not limited by the syntax or grammar of any particular language. This may well go some way towards explaining the attraction of the variety TV show *Circus,* which of course did not need to rely on a spoken language script but merely recorded the performers as they went through their act, whatever that might be, horse-riding, trapeze or hire-wire.

From 1974 onwards, while he was touring Mexico with the *Atayde Hermanos Circus*, Mr Atayde constantly urged Carlos to learn English, assuring him that he could make it very big in North America and that knowing the language would be put him at a tremendous advantage. But Carlos never had any real interest in speaking English, and so continued to drag his heels. Never the one to give up without a fight, Mr Atayde sought to reassure him further. He urged Carlos to try, and that he should really endeavour to make the effort to learn such a universally important language. Adding a carrot to his chastising stick by saying, "If you don't like it there (in the USA) just come back. We have a fine circus here. I like you, my family likes you. The crowds and the common people like you, and to us that is very, very important. So, do try." But even this level of encouragement fell on deaf ears and time continued to flow by with Carlos still not beginning to make the effort to learn some basic English words and phrases. Anyway, as the Mexican's say, "There was always tomorrow" - M*añana. Mañana.*

When he finally did get to the USA in 1978 and was working for Mr Hubert Castle, Carlos found that there was still no reason to learn English, for many of the people who worked for Mr Castle were themselves from South American and so Carlos was constantly surrounded by Mexicans and other Spanish speakers, who were only too keen to look after him. His Spanish speaking friends used to vie for the opportunity to help him, and he found he always had a ready escort if he wanted to go out of the circus grounds. Friends would turn up at the door of his caravan and announce, "Come Medina, Come. We're going to take you to the shops." And off they would go. So, Carlos, while living and working in one of the largest English speaking countries in the world, still shied away from learning the language. Although this did have its down side.

One day, while the Hubert Castle Circus was in Seattle, in Washington State, Carlos decided to venture out on his own. How difficult could it be to go round an American supermarket he thought? He had been round them countless times with his many Spanish speaking friends. It would be easy. No problem at all. So off he set. After wandering round a gargantuan retail edifice for some time he had managed to pick up a few tins of tuna fish paste and was looking forward to having a pleasant afternoon sandwich.

Back in his caravan he proudly lined up his newly purchased cans, along the side of the worktop, and began searching around for a tin-opener. As he was doing this, Mr Karl Linares, who was a wonderful old man, with a beautiful old-fashioned French poodle act, popped in to see him.

In the late nineteen fifties Karl had been a very famous high-wire artist but like others in that profession, had suffered a very serious fall, which put him out of action for quite some time. While he was recuperating, his wife Joyce bought some poodles and began to train them. Finding that he was unable to continue his previous career Karl joined his wife and went on to establish a very famous and highly successful dog act.

On entering the caravan, Karl's eyes alighted on the row of tins, proudly arrayed along the work-surface. Carlos caught Karl's eyes and followed them as they began to looked round the caravan in a very puzzled and odd way. Karl then shot a quick and even more puzzled look at Carlos. "Medina," he said at last, "Do you have a dog?"

"No." replied Carlos, totally confused about where this odd conversation might be going.

"Then why have you bought all this dog food?"

Carlos was mortified. So much for his ability to negotiate an American supermarket where the food was labelled in English. "I was going to make a sandwich, before the show. I thought it was fish paste. But I won't bother now..." he stammered, as his voice trailed off in embarrassment.

"But you must eat something." insisted the Great Linares. "Come. I'll take you out, and we'll get you some decent food."

Carlos resisted. "I'll be okay." he said.

Karl was outraged. "Medina," he chided, "You risk your life in the Roman Rings. You need something decent to eat. Don't be embarrassed, Medina, everybody has problems getting used to America. Don't worry about it." Then the kind old Mr Linares made a list of the items he thought Carlos would need for a sustaining meal, and they set off together to get them.

When they returned Mr Linares was particularly well placed to be able to dispose of the incriminating cans of evidence, and to his credit he never mentioned the incident ever again. However, it was still to be quite a few more years before Carlos built up the courage to try and master the English language.

With a year-long touring season behind him, and the addition of the cherry-topping of the television performance, by the end of 1978 Carlos was no doubt totally exhausted and possibly ready for a change. Hubert Castle too, was probably scouting around for a new star, as circuses thrive on change and the ability to draw in the crowds with ever new and exciting 'never-before-seen' acts so everyone was on the lookout for new options and opportunities.

Towards the end of the year Carlos had been approach by representatives from both the Ringland Brothers and the Barnum and Bailey Circus, two of the major circuses on the North American scene. Carlos was in the very fortunate position of being able to turn them both down, as he had already signed up to do a season with *Circus Vargas* who, at that time, even more fortunately for Carlos, were one of the best paying circuses in the world.

Chapter 9
CIRCUS VARGAS 1979

As the first few days of the New Year of 1979 began, Carlos took a new direction in his career. He had now left Hubert Castle and the Shriners behind, and had just taken up work with *Circus Vargas*, and its charismatic, and dynamic owner Clifford E Vargas.

Clifford E. Vargas was the son of Portuguese immigrants and was born and raised on a farm near Livermore, California, a fifty-minute drive from San Francisco. Further back in time his grandfather's generation had reputedly been circus owners in Portugal. As a child Clifford was fascinated with the circus and always cherished a dream that one day he would own his own show. He began working for several circuses and learned from the bottom up; handling the advertising, selling the tickets, being the doorman, tending to the animals and even, from time to time, serving as the ringmaster. Learning how each role worked enable him to have a clear understanding of how a circus functions and allowed him to shape and develop his unique vision of what a circus should be. In 1972, while he was working with the *Miller Johnson* circus it came up for sale, and Clifford immediately used his entire life-savings (reputedly $250,000) to purchase it; so began the process of realising his cherished childhood dream.

Clifford Vargas was a man with a mission. Having finally acquired the basic circus trappings he was determined to ensure that his circus would perform in a tent instead of following the then current fashion of hiring (the much cheaper) rented stadiums and auditoriums. He began the slow process of transforming the whole notion of what a circus was; buying more animals, commissioning a new, specially built tent, and turning the whole performing area into a three-ring circus spectacular. Complete with its new canvas, Circus Vargas reputedly became the world's largest three-ring circus performing under the big top and covering an area the size of a football field. Not only that, Clifford also came up with the unique idea of pitching his Big Top in the new shopping mall car parks that were then springing up across the USA, usually staying between three and four days before moving on.

It is worth considering the sheer complexity and effort required in moving a touring circus from one location to the next. In 1979 Circus Vargas was almost the size of a small town. Someone cleverly dubbed a circus as "*a city without a zip code*". At one point it included 150 animals, up to 300 employees and a theatre-style tent that could comfortably seat up to 1,500 people (although some accounts double this figure). It is also worth reflecting that it could take thirty men seven-hours to raise the Big Top, and then a few days later the same time to take it all back down again. Clearly Clifford Vargas was a man to be reckoned with.

Clifford Vargas not only had a burning vision but was also a very generous man with a big heart. One of the early performances Carlos gave with Circus Vargas was on 7th February 1979 as part of a special benefit performance in the parking lot of the Rancho Los Amigos Hospital in Downey, California, for patients and hospital staff, many of whom would never have seen a circus before, due to their physical disabilities and the care problems associated with looking after them. This was not just a token performance of one or two acts, for Clifford insisted that they saw the entire two-and-a-half-hour long show.

In a previous chapter we mentioned, when talking about the varying length of a circus season, that one of the factors that could affect the length of a stay was the weather. The day after the hospital performance - February 8th - Circus Vargas opened in Hawthorne California, one of the sprawl of suburbs that is Los Angeles. Carlos is again listed in the programme, but it is not the acts that were the stars on this occasion but the atrocious weather. Pouring rain pounded down on the Big Top and kept the local people away, resulting in the Circus being able to secure only 75% of its capacity audience. However, the show must go on and on it went, remaining and performing there until the 11th, before finally relocating to Rolling Hills, California.

Officially Circus Vargas opened their 1979 season in San Diego, California on January 5th, again amid heavy rain, and played in and around that area until January 15th. They also started that season with their brand-new tent. Carlos is mentioned as one the acts and is described as 'Robin Medina, Iron Jaw'. The next day - 16th January - the show was in Whittier, California before moving on to Burbank where it stayed until 21st January. After that the show moved on to tour round several other key cities in California State.

The Burbank performance was a key event for Circus Vargas and showed yet again Clifford Vargas at his most generous as he had set aside two full-length benefit performances with the proceeds going to the Gay Rights Movement. It was also a very important performance for Carlos as someone in the audience that day was about to change his life forever.

Carlos, casually attired, while working with Circus Vargas in 1979.

While Carlos was with *Las Truppe Algeciras* there was no need for him to be concerned about getting work or having an agent to look after his interests as his circus family were well known in South American and were in constant demand. When he set out on his own the issue of getting work clearly moved centre stage. Carlos was lucky in that Mr Atayde was keen to have him as part of his show, but as time went on Carlos began to pay more attention to the method and means by which performers were hired and contracted.

In South America most circuses were family affairs and as branches and new circuses emerged the act of managing them was bestowed upon the children and relatives of the original owners. A form of this system of nepotistic inheritance or expansion was also practice in relation to the acts the circus hired.

Circus Directors were constantly on the lookout for new and successful acts to add to their programmes and considered it as part of their job to spent some of their time visiting their 'rivals' or competitors to see what was on offer. When they saw an act they were interested in, they first approached spoke directly to the rival Circus Director to check out their prospective employees. Was the performer a moody person? Did they have a positive attitude? Were they a decent person? Did they have a good reputation with the crowd? So an informal background and personality check was conducted before the performer was even aware that he or she was on the transfer list!

In the case of Carlos getting work was relatively easy. Carlos had a good reputation. Directors said of Mr Medina that he was always very smart, always very elegant, that he integrated well into the circus, that he was not moody, and that no one had ever had any problems with him. So, for Carlos, the word of mouth, Director to Director, method of getting work had served him well and he had never thought seriously about getting an agent, but that was about to change.

That Clifford Vargas was gay was well known, his flamboyant manner and extravagantly expensive gold and diamond jewellery attested to it. It is therefore no surprise to learn of his desire to use his power and influence to help the gay community. As mentioned above he used the Burbank performance to advance that cause. The 'Circus Report' from February 12, 1979 issue Number 7 records the event in the following way:

" On the second day, during its Burbank showing. Circus Vargas gave two benefit performances for the Gay Rights Movement involving The Gay Metropolitan Community Church and the Gey (sic) Community Service Club. 3,500 gays attended the first showing. A like number attended the second. I am told the audience was one of the most enthusiastic Circus Vargas has ever played to, with standing ovations for performers, and with aerialist ROBIN MEDINA the "hit" of the show."

As well as being the star of the show and receiving a tumultuous standing ovation, no doubt accompanied by cacophonous shrieks and screams, Carlos had also been given another honour. It was traditional in the circus world for a star performer to be given the most prominent spot in the middle of the ring. Normally this went to a famous and glamorous young lady - often a famous trapeze artist. It was very unusual to see a man occupy this 'sacred' spot, but Carlos had nailed it. On that occasion Carlos recalls, finding the whole recollection highly amusing, "I was wearing big feathers and presumably looked more like a woman, than anything else!"

After the show Clifford Vargas was very keen for Carlos to meet a guest who had come to see the show, a certain Billy Arata. Billy Arata had begun his career as a circus performer and developed a very famous hire wire act. Later in his career he had married Margaret

Hampson and together they had established *Hampsons (Theatrical) Agency*, based in Birmingham, England. Billy thenceforth spent his time travelling the world looking for new acts to add to their portfolio. After seeing the Burbank show, Billy was determine to sign Carlos up, but he was also fascinated by some of the events he had seen that afternoon.

He quizzed Carlos about how he had managed to get the centre stage spot and seemed totally amazed that a man could ever be elevated to that coveted and exalted position. Carlos also had his own view of Billy's interest in him. By that time Carlos' hair was back to its natural shiny black state. Long gone was the platinum blonde 'Viking' look. Carlos, when reporting his first meeting with Billy, had his tongue firmly in his cheek saying archly, "Mr Arata didn't care about my act. He was only interested in my jet-black hair. He was infatuated by it!"

Joking apart, Billy Arata was obviously very keen to add Carlos to his list of acts and told Carlos that he would give him his address and contact details and send him a telegram offering him a role in a circus in Europe. Never, in all his time with circuses had Carlos ever considered that he would go to Europe, yet, here was a well-known, and well respected Theatrical Agent, from one of the most successful circus agencies in the world, offering him a potential contract to work in Europe. Not only that, he was proposing sending Carlos to Norway. Norway in Scandinavia! Carlos loved the idea, all those blonde haired, blue-eyed young men! Even though Mr Arata had promised to send a telegram soon confirming all this, and even though Carlos was very keen to go, he decided to remain prudent and wait and see what transpired.

About three and half months later, true to his word, a telegram arrived for Mr Vargas. On receipt of it Mr Vargas came rushing over to find Carlos and, almost beside himself with excitement, explained to him that Billy Arata had sent a telegram and wanted to know if he was still interested in going to Scandinavia. Clifford explained that Mr Arata was going to pay for the hotel in Norway for the first three months, and after that the Circus Director there, would provide Carlos with a caravan, along with a driver, to take him from town to town as they toured round the country. The increasingly excited Cliff Vargas read on, explaining it was a very, very good salary. One hundred dollars per day! Less of course, 25% for the agent and 10% for Norwegian tax.

Mr Vargas said, "You should go Carlos. It will be something different for you. You will like the countryside. They are all Vikings over there. You should go!" He then looked at Carlos and said, "You are gay. Maybe you will find your prince charming over there."

Although delighted by the amazing offer, as well as the possibility of finding his own prince charming, Carlos was more worried about the travel details. The itinerary that had arrived with the telegram showed the route as going from Los Angeles to New York, then New York to Oslo. Carlos explained to Cliff that he was terrified by the idea of flying all the way to New York on his own. Would it not be possible to fly directly from Los Angeles? As the proposed journey was still several months away Clifford said he would contact his travel agent and find out what was available. However, he did stress to Carlos that he would need to arrive in Norway at least ten days before the season started.

After the excitement of the Burbank performances and the rapidly materialising promise of a contract to travel to Europe, Carlos went back to work and tried to focus on his daily performance, rehearsing and stretching and keeping himself in tip-top physical condition.

One day while going through his rehearsal routine Carlos was approached by a woman called Anna Delmonte. Anna was one of the many people who made up the vast extended family or staff of Circus Vargas. She was the seamstress for the circus, making and repairing the costumes used by the various acts. She had come to see Carlos in order to persuade him to help her train her young son, Rudolph. The Delmonte family were originally from Holland but had been based in the States for several years. Rudolph was born in Sarasota, in Florida, a city that became known as 'Circus City' due to the fact that the *Ringland Brothers Circus* was based there during the winter and consequently attracted a large number of circus artists who took up residence there with their families.

Anna Delmonte was clearly an ambitious lady and wanted the very best for her son. It seems Rudolph had been taught ballet, how to play the piano, and a crude form of contortionism from a very early age. Not content with being taught basic skills, by the age eight, he had been performing in private clubs and at parties in and around the Sarasota area. Anna wanted Carlos to teach Rudolph to be a contortionist. Always the opportunist it seems, she wanted Carlos to teach him specifically how to be a dental aerial contortionist, because very few performers do an iron jaw act and therefore there would be a greater chance of success for her young son.

Carlos agreed, and was introduced to Rudolph who was about nine years old at the time. Presumably in a poignant echo of Carlos' own early 'performance' back in Cúcuta in front of the people who were destined to become his circus family, young Rudolph went through a little sequence of bends and twist before Carlos, to show off his skills and abilities. His body was very soft and pliable and he wasn't sure how to improve on what he could already do. Carlos watched him and quickly ascertained that he was a chest contortionist, being able to flex from his sternum. He also noticed that he was able to dislocate parts of his legs and lower body. After watching this short performance Carlos thought that Rudolph most certainly could be trained and agreed he would try and teach him some basic moves.

The following day Carlos began to squeeze and gently push and hold the eager young boy into new positions in order to make his cartilages more malleable. He also explained to the boy that he should not be alarmed if he urinated on himself, or even on Carlos, as apparently this was a common side-effect when the body is forced into unusual and somewhat unnatural positions. As Rudolph was already very flexible, and now having a competent teacher, he made rapid progress.

After several days, Carlos explained to him a new sequence of movements. Rudolph was to stand with his arms at his side and slowly raise them up so that they were parallel to the ground. However, he was to work against the natural tendency of the shoulders to rise up and instead to work strenuously to hold them down. The boy started straight away and worked very diligently and strenuously. After he had gone through the sequence twenty to thirty times Carlos told him he had done enough for the day, and that his level of effort and concentration was very good

Rudolph was clearly very highly motivated as well as being a very quick learner and within five days he had managed to master all the basic skills that Carlos was keen to impart. He was so excited that he had learned to do so much so quickly that he broke down and cried and kissed Carlos thanking him profusely. Reflecting back on this event Carlos was typically philosophical, "Many people have helped me in my life", he said, "so I was very happy to be able to give something back".

As Rudolph's mother wanted him to learn to be a Dental Act the next thing to do was to find a dentist to make a bit for his mouth. The mouth-piece is used as a training tool, to keep the head in place, strengthen the teeth and mouth grip, and enable the rest of the body to be manipulated and pushed and pulled in order to make it more subtle and flexible. The mouth bit is traditionally made from leather and for contortion purposes needs to be made of pig leather because it's much stronger than either horse or cow leather. Pigskin will also not cause any infections or other side effects which horse and cow leather sometimes can. So, in order to get him a mouth-piece, Carlos and Rudolph went looking for a dentist.

Through word of mouth they quickly found a reputable one near to where the Big Top was pitched and Carlos was very impressed by the skill and intelligence of this particular American dentist. Carlos explained to him what it was they were after and he was very quickly able and willing to help. He first took several casts of the boy's mouth and had him clench his teeth in order to get a mould of his grip, and within a few days had made up a perfect cast. The next step was to get the leather bit prepared. They managed to find a horse trainer in the vicinity, who reputedly made goods from horse leather. When they met he struck Carlos as a very eccentric character indeed. It then transpired that he was completely fascinated by the circus and everything to do with it. When he heard of their requirements, he too, like the dentist, was very keen to help. He had, of course, never been asked to make anything remotely like this out of leather before but, having been given the cast from the dentist, and following Carlos's descriptions of what was required said he would see what he could do.

After a few days he turned up at Carlos' caravan, star-struck to be among all the circus paraphernalia. He had brought the mouth piece and was ready for Rudolph to try it. From his own experience Carlos thought it best to forewarn Rudolph of possible side-effects. When Carlos had been trained, his circus family had never bothered to have a dental impression made, or a proper pattern for the mouth grip created. Carlos commented that his own original mouth grip was far too big for him and completely filled up his mouth making him look like a 'swollen jawed monkey'. He had taken a very long time to get used to it. Carlos was therefore keen to prepare Rudolph for this possibility, explaining to him that when he first began to bite down on the bit, it would be a strange and terrible experience, he would feel sick, maybe even be sick, but eventually he would become accustomed to it.

So, with his whole family anxiously gathered around to see him try it for the first time, it was a pleasant shock for everyone when an excited young Rudolph announced that it felt very comfortable in his mouth, indeed it was a perfect fit! He was able to bite down on it without any discomfort whatsoever. Carlos was both relieved and impressed and urged Anna to get two or three extra pieces made, as possible backups, as such a high level of craftsmanship was a very rare thing indeed.

Rudolph Delmonte performing later in his career.

With the mouth piece complete they were then able to move on to the next stage of the training. Using the mouth piece Rudolph was able to grip it tightly while Carlos slowly began to introduce some of the basic contortions that they had worked on, but now with

Rudolph much more stationary, Carlos was able to apply much more pressure and therefore bend the boy's body further than they had done before. It was not long before Rudolph was well on his way to developing an effective sequence of contortions which could be easily moulded into an entertaining act. Yet again Carlos was very impressed by how well the boy did, first in learning to cope with the dental grip, and then mastering the more painful exercises that followed. Reflecting back on his own career Carlos worked out that it took him about a month to learn what the boy had picked up in a mere five days!

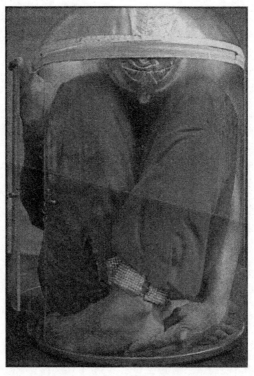

Hugo Zamoratte - 'the man in the bottle

As Carlos had suspected it transpired that Rudolph was not just a contortionist, but also a dislocator, someone who has the ability to dislocate his bones and then relocate them, which is really quite a different skill-set from contortionism. Later in his career Rudolph went on to learn the art of dislocation from a friend of Carlos', Zamoratte, an Argentinean contortionist and dislocator, also known as '*the man in the bottle*'.

Young Rudolph later took up the stage name of "Rudolph Pinky Delmonte" and went on to be a very successful performer, performing with the *Ringling Brothers Circus* and *Barnum & Bailey Circus,* as well as doing a season in Las Vegas performing alongside *Siegfried & Roy* at the Desert Inn. Videos of some of his performances can still be found on YouTube.

Carlos was very happy to have been able to help advance the career of this young man and to impart to him some of the skills he himself had worked so hard to acquire. Rudolph's family too were very pleased and impressed with the work that Carlos had done, and were very generous to Carlos for the remainder of his season with *Circus Vargas*.

Carlos's season was however to come to a dramatic end. Circus Report in its 29th October 1979 edition describes what happened:

AT last I have details on the ROBIN MEDINA deportation. The aerialist was with the Castle show last season and with Circus Vargas this year. Apparently he was working without proper papers and authorities caught up to him and sent him back to Colombia. LOS GAUCHOS (with C.V.) spearheaded a movement to collect funds to assist the performer, put up his bail and sent the remaining money to him. The performer has an engegemant (sic) pending in Europe but when he was arrested his

trailer and vehicle were confiscated along with his rigging.
Performers with C.V. are now attempting to get his rigging and
ship it to him so he can resume working.

As in all walks of life jealousy can raise its ugly green
head at any time and inspire some cruel and despicable
behaviour. The circus world is no different and possibly
one where jealousy is more likely to arise, as success or
failure in that world depends not just on one's abilities
but on one's reputation and reception by the crowd.

Towards the beginning of autumn that year, Clifford
Vargas had informed Carlos that he wanted him to go
to Monte Carlo to represent Circus Vargas at the
prestigious, *International Circus Festival of Monte-Carlo* in
December. Carlos was of course delighted by such an
honour and could not wait to attend and perform on
behalf of his friend. The news was supposed to be kept
secret but before too long, and given what we have
already learned about that close-knit world, it was all
round the circus.

It appears that when this information entered the ears
of another aerial act then travelling with the Circus, it
acted like the poison on Hamlet's father. Although it
did not quite kill them, it did engender thoughts of
death. They felt insulted and slighted, and were furious
that they had not been selected for the honour of
representing *Circus Vargas* in Monte-Carlo. Such was
their level of jealousy that they contrived to have Carlos
reported to the police, claiming that his papers were not
in order. Whether they had inside knowledge about this
we do not know but the police, acting on this tip-off,
were obliged to check Carlos' papers. It transpired that
through an unfortunate administrative oversight they
had indeed expired and the police had no option but to

deport him, thus bringing to a rather undignified end his highly successful season with *Circus Vargas*.

Chapter 10

TEN YEARS IN THE AIR 1980-1989

Finding himself rather abruptly and surprisingly back in South America for the latter months of 1979, Carlos was unsure quite what to do. His contract with Billy Arata had already come through along with all the details of his trip to Norway in April 1980, but that was still several months away. However, his triumph in the USA had not gone unnoticed south of the border and Carlos was soon approached by Mr Razzore, the Director of *Gran Circo Razzore*. His family circus was currently touring in Venezuela and Mr Razzore was very keen to engage the now famous and crowd-pulling 'American Star' Robin Medina as part of his show. Given the long delays in securing visas to re-enter the USA, now that he could no longer rely on the power of the Shriners, Carlos thought it highly unlikely that he would be able to return to the States before his trip to Europe, so he was very happy to accept this kind offer.

Carlos toured with *Gran Circo Razzore* for several months, visiting the major towns and cities of his home country of Venezuela and was generally greeted with rapturous applause. Unfortunately, just before he was about to cut back on his performances and begin to prepare himself for his trip to Norway, Carlos had the second major fall in his career. The circus had been performing in Barquisimeto, the fourth largest city in Venezuela and an important industrial and commercial centre, when he lost his balance and fell to the ground. He was taken to the hospital where he remained receiving treatment for three or four days.

Sadly the history of Gran Circo Razzore is also somewhat blighted with bad luck. Established in Rio de Janeiro, Brazil in 1836, almost a whole generation of the Razzore family perished in a terrible tragedy, in 1948. At that time the Circus, which had been based in Cuba, was on its way to Columbia. They were travelling in what appears to have been a very old and somewhat inadequate ship, the Euzquera, when it was hit by a hurricane and sank almost immediately. Of the 57 people on board 46 were members of the circus. Twelve people did survive the wreck but the majority of those were members of the Cuban Crew. Nearly all the Circus performers and members of the Razzore family, all the animals, and all the equipment perished in that tragic and freak accident. Emilio Razzore, the then owner and director of the circus, was one of the few crucial survivors as he had flown ahead to prepare for the arrival of the Circus in Columbia. This tragedy clearly took its toll on the family but Emilio later remarried and was able, over time, to rebuild the circus to its former glory.

Luckily for Carlos the fall was not a major one and he had only twisted his ankle, but it was still significant enough that it would take about three to four weeks to heal fully. Carlos was very anxious about this, as he needed to keep performing to earn money so he could save towards his Norwegian trip. He approached the Circus Director's daughter, Erika Razzore, who was a good friend of his. He explained his financial predicament to her and she spoke to her father. The Razzore family very quickly and generously agreed to pay Carlos one hundred dollars per week, which was sufficient to covered his hotel bill and other needs until he got better. Mr Razzore, in particular, was incredibly supportive, when he heard of Carlos' distress. He immediately came to see him, and reassured him they would help him in whatever way they could. He was adamant that Carlos focus on getting back into good physical shape for his Norwegian trip and then became very paternal offering to lend him five hundred dollars to help him get established in the early stages of his Scandinavian tour, agreeing that Carlos could pay him back when he returned.

Mr Razzore, seemed particularly proud of Carlos and his achievements and insisted, " You need to go to Norway. You must go and represent Venezuela. For us, South Americans it is a very big thing to go to Europe. Not many people get invited to play in Norway. Go. Go."

Much relieved by this generosity and support, Carlos was able to then focus on recuperating, and getting himself back into tip-top physical condition ready for his forthcoming trip to the land of fjords.

In the Spring of 1980 Carlos travelled to Norway to work with *Cirkus Merano* - Norway's National Circus, based in Oslo. The opening night of the Norwegian performance was 23rd April 1980, and Carlos had been instructed to get there ten days before the season started in order to acclimatize himself so he set off on 1st April flying from Caracas in Venezuela through to Oslo, Norway.

Leaving the heat and warm sunshine of Caracas, Carlos, although very excited at the prospect of performing in Europe, had not really given much thought to what Norway would look like. For him it was just another engagement, another circus, another place to perform. He knew and was totally confident in his ability to do his part in the show wherever that show might be located, and he was now fully recovered from his recent fall. It was with some shock and a degree of consternation that as the plane landed in Norway on the 2nd April that he looked out of the window and could see nothing but snow. There were no blonde, blued-eyed Viking princes anywhere to be seen: just white, white, endlessly white, pristine acres of pure white snow, with more falling and copiously adding to it.

Having eventually recovered from this first impression of this new country Carlos was met at the airport and helped to check into his hotel. This involved him having to bluff his language skills in the hope that by means of signs, hand gestures, and furtive turning of the pages of a Spanish - English dictionary he might somehow make himself understood.

Although he had landed in Oslo - the Norwegian capital -   the first city the Circus played at was Trondheim 300 miles to the north. Carlos' nationality often seems to have been a source of speculation, and the *Cirkus Merano* programme for 1980 has a picture of Carlos but identifies him as coming from Nicaragua! (*A Database covering Scandinavian circuses from 1900 until today lists him as Robin Medina, an Acrobatic, performing with Merano in1980, but contradictorily shows his country of origin as being the USA.*) The *Merano* programme, sporting a picture of Carlos attired completely in white and hanging by one knee, refers to him as the 'Snake Man'.

One can imagine from the point of view of the audience gazing up into the heights of the Big Top the writhing and spinning white figure stretching and twisting between the two Roman Rings could well appear snake-like, as he slithered and glided at great speed between the various set-poses of his routine. The programme goes on to refer to him as being the star of the Circus Vargas show the previous season and notes that Circus Vargas is 'America's largest tent circus'. The blurb finally goes on to reassure the audience that they will never have seen anything remotely like this before!

The season with *Cirkus Merano* lasted seven months, and after an initially period of living in hotels, the Circus Director purchased a mobile caravan and allocated Carlos a designated driver, and so it was, in this familiar fashion that Carlos lived and toured with the Circus up and down the length and breadth of Norway, from April to October 1980.

Carlos in 1980 hanging by his teeth while performing for the Cirkus Merano in Norway. (Canobbio on the canvas, is the name of a famous Big Top manufacturer from Milan.)

An arrangement, which was soon to become a regular feature of their relationship together, was that shortly before the final days of the season Billy Arata would fly out to where Carlos was performing to see him, check that everything was OK, and inform him about his next engagement. On this occasion Carlos was in Oslo when Billy arrived, and informed him that he had two choices of where to go next. The first choice was for Carlos to fly to Holland and perform in the country of Queen Beatrice or, he could go to Spain and perform for King Carlos De bourbon. "Well, of course, I chose the Spanish option." Carlos informed me archly.

After the *Cirkus Merano* season ended there were still a few weeks before he was due to fly out to Madrid and so Carlos flew to England and stayed as a guest of Billy Arata and Margaret Hampson at their spacious home off the Hamstead Road, in the leafy, tree-lined suburb of Handsworth in Birmingham. Billy and Margaret were to play host to Carlos between shows right up until 1993.

The Spanish show was scheduled to last for twenty-five days over the Christmas period. It took place in the *Palacio de Los Deportes de Madrid* (Palace of Sport) and was part of the 9th *Festival Mundial del Circo*. Having arrived there, Carlos was once again caught out by strange European customs and practices. This time it was not snow that had thrown him, but the fact that there were three shows a day and that the first show began at eleven thirty in the morning. It transpired that this early show was dedicated to charity with an audience composed of disadvantaged and disabled adults and children. Having realised what was required Carlos quickly adapted to this new convention, and before long was giving his all to ensure that those who saw him went away with at least a glimpse of some otherworldly hope in their hearts.

While performing in Madrid, late one evening after the day's performances were over, Carlos was approached by a stranger, who came straight to the point and asked him who his agent was? Carlos, slightly taken aback, quickly informed him that his agent was Billy Arata, from Hampsons Theatrical Agency, to which the gentleman, of seemingly very few words, replied, "Ahh. Thank you very much." and departed.

It was not until Billy Arata arrived towards the last few day of the Spanish show that Carlos learned that the tight lipped gentleman was a certain Mr W. H. Wilkie, originally from Liverpool, and now a millionaire and also the owner of both of the world famous Circus Wilkies. The two circuses - one called *Wilkies International Circus* and the other run by his son Robert called *Robero's Circus* - were the only two circuses then performing in South Africa. It transpired that after his abrupt exchange with Carlos he had telephoned Billy Arata straight away from his hotel room in Madrid and engaged Carlos to perform in South Africa for the 1981 season, and a new contract was quickly drawn up.

The new contract specified that the hiring organisation would pay for the cost of transporting Carlos' luggage. Carlos did not travel lightly. His luggage was very heavy indeed, weighing in at nearly 275 kg - some 606lbs! Carlos explained that this extraordinary weight was because he had so many costumes. He elaborated further, "The audience was crazy for me. They loved my changes of clothes, and I had so many, many, wonderful costumes! And of course, the circus directors were very happy to pay for the cost of all this luggage. They were millionaires!"

Carlos (now aged 30) executing a perfect full length splits, high up above the crowds while working for Robero's Circus in Johannesburg, South Africa in 1981.

Shortly after the Spanish show, and in a strange irony, given events at the end of his stint with Circus Vargas, Carlos flew with Billy to Monte Carlo, to perform for two days in the annual Circus Festival established and presided over by Princess Grace of Monaco which we will return to in the next chapter. After Monte Carlo,

Carlos returned to the UK and closed 1980 with a three and a half week season with the *Sally Chipperfield Circus* (Sally was the daughter of Dick Chipperfield Senior from the famous Chipperfield circus dynasty) at Bingley Hall in Birmingham.

South Africa in 1981, - Carlos at his flamboyant best. Revealing both the showman and the extrovert. Here he is in the Grand Parade at the start of the show receiving the applause and adulation of the audience while attired in a subtle, totally off-the-shoulder, number, with a fetching understated feather hat.

In late February 1981 Carlos set off to join the newly established *Robero's Circus* in the still apartheid-riven

South African city of Johannesburg. He was to tour with them for the rest of year. Circus Report for August 3rd 1981 (characteristically misspelling the name of the circus owner) notes: *"ROBIN MEDINA, cloud swing performer, is presently touring with the Boswell-Witkie Circus in South Africa."*

Carlos clearly had fun in South Africa, and was fully able to expose the exhibitionist side of his character as the above photo shows. Robero's programme for that season dubs Carlos: "The Queen (?) of the air - Robin Medina".

Unlike the United Kingdom at the time, South Africa seemed to lap up Carlos' sexual ambiguity and extravagant cross dressing. Carlos informed me that the Ring Master used to announce his performance in the following way.'We cannot bring you Mirriam Gordi, but we do have Mr Robin Medina, Queen of the Air!'

Mirriam Gordi was well-known in South Africa at the time. He was a German transvestite and his flouncing and excessive femininity, and lavish use of highly ornate costumes, made the comparison particularly apt.

South Africa was also to be the place that Carlos made his first serious effort to grapple with the English Language. He had been dabbling with this new tongue while in Norway but as time wore on he began to realise that he really had arrived in Europe and would probably never leave. Billy and Margaret were assuming the role of his new protectors, almost his new family, and so Carlos at last set his mind to speaking English, even though it was to be spoken with a thick Spanish accent.

In 1982 Carlos was working for and travelling with the *Gerry Cottle Circus*. Gerry Cottle had long since sold this particular circus and the current owners were merely capitalizing on the successful '*Cottle*' brand name. They were on a tour of East Asia and the Macau performance was something of an unusual assignment in that the Circus was just one part of a much larger attraction - a permanent funfair. Carlos later recalled that it was similar to the arrangement which prevailed at Chessington Zoo, which also had a permanent funfair set in the grounds. The Chessington Zoo funfair had been set up and run by Coco the Clown's daughter, Tamara, who was an old friend of Carlos.

The funfair in Macau was somewhat more exotic than that at Chessington Zoo, and possibly an early precursor to that territory's recently built *Fisherman's Wharf* theme park. Macau was situated across the Pearl River Delta from Hong Kong. At that time Macau was legally regarded as "a Chinese territory under (temporary) Portuguese administration". It was finally handed back to the Chinese in 1999. The island was best known for its gambling, and was said to dwarf Las Vegas as a gambling hub. The place oozed with atmosphere, was full of bustling street markets where vendors sold food of every conceivable kind, and one's eyes were constantly startled by the strange mingling of the old and new, thanks to hundreds of years of fusion between European and Chinese cultures.

When circuses were travelling in foreign countries, in this case Hong Kong, China and Malaysia, it was common for the star acts to have their nation's Ambassador invited to come and see the show. Macau was no different and an invitation had been extended, on Carlos' behalf, to the Venezuelan Ambassador. The Ambassador had replied almost immediately, indicating that he would be delighted to come and see the show. It was also part of the protocol for the Ambassador, at some point during their tour, to invite all the acts back to the Embassy for a reception. So, after one particular evening performance, which the Ambassador had attended, the circus performers were ferried across the city to the Venezuelan Embassy, where they were formally welcomed and thanked by the highly enthusiastic plenipotentiary of Venezuela.

When he was introduced to Carlos he was very effusive with his praise of the performance and then, presumably infected by the cheeky camp of Carlos, said, "I knew that we in Venezuela have some of the most beautiful women in the world but I did not realize, until now, that we have the most beautiful gay man I've ever seen in my life!" This was much to Carlos' delight, and the loud titters of approval of the other members of the show.

After completing the 1982 Asian tour, Carlos moved permanently to England. He continued to live with Billy and Margaret, renting a room from them. Billy was finding Carlos plenty of work in the thriving UK Circus circuit and he and Margaret, finally convinced Carlos to buy a car and caravan.

Despite his reluctance to learn and his fear of the macho side of himself that driving might bring out, the Cuban driver from the Hubert Castle days finally got his wish, and Carlos learned to drive. Carlos used the car and caravan to travel round the UK staying close to the circus he was then performing with. He was able to park near the Big Top and to sleep and eat in his caravan for the duration of the show, before driving on as part of the circus convoy to the next engagement.

Carlo's car and caravan parked near to the big top when travelling with Circus Hoffman in 1984

Carlos was thus to spend the next five or six years of his life touring the length and breadth of the UK. He did occasionally perform in Europe again but was now mostly based in England and performing for some of the most prestigious Circuses in the country. During 1984 for instance we find Carlos performing for the Circus Hoffman which, at that time, was the biggest circus in the UK.

In 1986-7 Carlos worked for the world-famous Chipperfield Circus. This time it was for the two brothers, Tommy and Charles Chipperfield. Carlos had been contracted to performed for them when they were presenting an indoor show at the world famous *Blackpool Tower Circus.* The picture below - taken from the circus programme - shows Carlos on the Roman Rings against the ornate background of the Tower Circus ballroom.

A season at the Blackpool Tower Circus normally lasted about six months, and this prestigious contract came about through a joint venture by Carlos' agent Billy Arata and a very flamboyant and famous theatrical agent, Roberto Germains who was well known on the Circus scene and his agency had a prestigious office in central London, in Denmark Street, just off Oxford Circus. Mr Germains also had the unique distinction of having appeared in the 1983 James Bond movie, *Octopussy,* playing the character of the 'Ring Master'. It seemed that Arata and Germains had done a deal together, to 'share' Carlos, in order that he could perform with the *Chipperfields* at the *Blackpool Tower Circus.* This arrangement proved a very successful one for all concerned

In 1988, Carlos was travelling with the *Courtney Brothers Circus* in the County of Galway in Southern Ireland. Clearly the flamboyant and ambiguous nature of Carlos' sexuality was irrepressible, and seemed to have fascinated the people of Southern Ireland. During the week of the show's visit to the region, the local newspaper (I believe) the *Tuam Herald,* posted an article under a headline which had clearly required a great deal of thought: "Circus in Tuam this weekend". The article does a quick preview of what attractions the circus holds in store, but the bulk of the very short article is about Carlos:

"...one of the great "mystery" attractions is the world-famous Medina, half-man half-woman or vice versa. This person (single/plural) will come under the expert scrutiny of well know entrepreneur Tom McNally, who at one stage of his varied career was a master of prestidigitation. Anyone who can fool Tom is worthy of a prize..."

We do not hear the outcome of Mr MacNally's investigations, but can feel reassured that whatever they were, they helped draw the local crowds to the big top in the hope of making up their own minds. Later in the tour Carlos had yet another fall, this time in Connemara. Luckily it was not serious and resulted only in a sprain and some minor bruising. Fortunately Carlos had not been very high off the ground at the time.

Towards the end of 1989 Carlos was contracted to perform for the *Circus Carl Busch* in Cologne in Germany where he was based for four months. Unlike the UK where a Circus is constantly on the move, in Germany they tend to be based in the same city for the duration of their season. We will return to this engagement a little later. Having looked in on the performance side of Carlos' career, let us see what else was happening in his life during this time.

Chapter 11

FAMOUS PEOPLE

It's difficult now to imagine a world without televisions, tablets, mobile phones, X-boxes, DVDs and Blue Rays and all the other paraphernalia that we have at our disposal to entertain ourselves. Yet, at the time Carlos was beginning to emerge onto the circus landscape, the world was a much simpler place. The circus still represented a major force in the world of entertainment, and Carlos was a bright luminous star slowly rising to the firmament of that sparkling and exotic world. One such perk of any form of stardom is that other people are eager to bask in your achievements. They want to meet you and more importantly they want to tell their friends they met you. Not only that, they want to tell their friends that they knew you intimately, and regularly wined and dined with you, regardless of the veracity of their tale. As *Las Truppe Algecidas* toured around South America they were often invited to the homes of the rich, famous and powerful who wanted to be seen as gracious hosts, personal friends or sometimes on rare occasions as just fellow performers.

Richard Burton and Elizabeth Taylor – 1963

In 1963 Richard Burton was playing the part of the Reverend Dr. T. Lawrence Shannon in the film version of *The Night of the Iguana* which was being filmed in locations in and around the Puerto Vallarta area on the west coast of Mexico. Ava Gardner, Deborah Kerr, and Sue Lyon also starred in the film. The playwright Tennessee Williams was part of the entourage also, no doubt observing closely the work of the director, John

Huston, who had written the screenplay from Williams' original stage play. This illustrious band, along with the vast crew of supporting actors and technicians required in the making of a film, were based in Mexico for approximately three months that summer. Although not appearing in the film, Elizabeth Taylor was also in Puerto Vallarta, pursuing her now very public affair with Richard Burton. They were both still married to other partners at the time so it was causing quite a scandal. The tabloids, took great delight in reporting the off-screen activities of the infamous pair. During the filming the Burtons lived in a rented house called "Casa Kimberley" which Richard Burton later bought, and it was here, in late 1963, that Carlos met them.

Carlos' circus family were touring Mexico that year, and were performing for several days in Puerto Vallarta. In Mexico at that time there were about 40-45 circuses regularly touring around the country and all competing with each other. These tended to be circus families where, through nepotistic succession the extended circus family had create a network of separate circuses.

While Richard Burton and the others were engaged in the filming process, and keen to sample the local culture for herself, Elizabeth Taylor, decided to visit the circus. When the Circus Director saw her he refused to allow her to pay, and she was treated like royalty and escorted to a first class seat at the side of the ring. After the performance she graciously invited the troupe back to her house for a light snack later that evening.

Richard Burton joined them shortly after they arrived and he and Taylor welcomed them, appreciated them as fellow performers and treating them civilly and with respect. They put on no airs and graces despite their famous stature. Carlos, although only thirteen at the time, found Elizabeth Taylor to be a simple human being, and a very lovely and beautiful lady. Indeed a classical English lady!

Carlos (aged 13) with his sisters left to right Sonia, Alcina & Marlene and unknown man

Both Burton and Taylor spoke excellent Spanish (Burton owned a large tract of land in Spain) and Carlos was able to follow the conversation with ease. Richard Burton seemed particularly fascinated by Tito Gandhi and quickly steered the conversation towards talk of his life and work. Burton had met him recently and was delighted to learn that he spoke English as he had worked in North America for several years. Burton with his rich hypnotic voice extolled the virtues and skill of Gandhi who was at the time one of the most famous horse trainers in Latin America. He trained horses to perform dressage and Burton seemed totally fascinated by the process of educating horses to perform in that way. Despite already seeming to have a wealth of knowledge about his subject Burton also asked his guests many questions about him, and the methods he used. He was also keen to hear about Gaiman, a Welsh Village that had been established near Buenos Aires. Apparently in 1865, 150 people had emigrated from Wales to set up new religious colony in Argentina where they sought to protect their lifestyle which had become endangered in their native Wales. Burton again seemed fascinated by these people and their activities and was keen to learn more about this exotic link to the land of his birth.

Carlos revelled in all this, and keenly observed the entire goings on in complete, but reverent silence. As he was still only a young boy, he was kept to the back, where he was able to watch in fascinated adoration. He observed from a distance standing next to his sisters, very much one of the girls, while his mother kept a puzzled, hawk-like eye on him, to ensure he was behaving, and no doubt wondering why a young boy, who should, by rights, be totally bored by all this, was finding it all so fascinating and absorbing.

Such was the life of a circus performer in those days, that they were able to mix and mingle freely and on equal terms with probably the highest paid and most 'infamous' couple in the world. Visits like this one were clearly a high spot, but during most tours someone of wealth, fame or power would be keen to invite the family back after the show, to provide some modest snacks, some light and polite conversation and to bask in the reflected glow of their stardom if only for a short period of time.

Michael York – 1967

While the family were performing in Lima in Peru in 1967 Carlos met Michael York, who was apparently there to make a film about the Incas for the Peruvian Government. By that time York had already starred in the BBC's 'The Forsyte Saga' and risen to international fame playing the character of Brian Roberts, in Bob Fosse's film of 'Cabaret' starring opposite Liza Minnelli's, Sally Bowles.

After the show, Michael York came to meet Carlos. The meeting would not have lasted for very long. Like all meetings with famous celebrities who came 'back stage' after the show, the Circus Director would firstly have asked them not to disturb or molest the performers, pointing out that they would be tired after their performance and needed time to relax and wind down. However, despite this polite warning the first thing Michael York did on entering the tent was to grip Carlos' forearm very tightly with both his hands. Then he touched Carlos' chest, feeling two or three ribs with his fingers. Clearly somewhat surprised by the solidity of Carlos' body, York uttered, "You have a bone!"

With Michael York - 1967

Somewhat taken aback, but at the same time highly amused, and completely un-phased, Carlos replied, 'Yes, I have a bone.' and began to touch his arms, ribs and other parts of his body to indicate the reality of the underlying bone structure. It seems that Michael York had been so impressed while watching Carlos perform and seeing how flexible and pliable Carlos' body appeared to be, that he had somehow conceived the rather naïve idea that Carlos had no bones in his body! Carlos was 17 at the time and Michael York would have been around 25 but Carlos felt no qualms about exposing this rather foolish notion in such a humorous and cheeky way. This native naivety displayed by York, was a possible reason that he was able to create and portray so well the superbly naïve character of 'Brian Roberts' (claimed by some to be the Christopher Isherwood character) in the film of Cabaret.

Juan Perón - President of Argentina– 1974

Despite the dangers of his profession and the huge numbers of audience members who were likely to be watching him perform at any given time, Carlos confessed to having been nervous only twice in his life. The second time was when he met Grace Kelly in Monaco in 1980, but the first, and probably most extreme state of nervousness was produced when he met Juan Perón, President of Argentina, in 1974 at the tender age of 24, not long after he had embarked on his solo career. Not only was he nervous he was petrified!

In retrospect 1974 was probably not a good year to visit Argentina. The more famous Perón, Eva, had already been dead some 22 years (she died in 1952) but her memory lingered on. Juan Perón began his third term as President on October 12, 1973, swept to power with a 62% majority, but by then he was reputedly seriously ill. There are those who suggest that he may very well have been senile by that time, due to the severity of the various illnesses that beset him. The country was in turmoil and Perón had only secured his return to office through complex political machinations, worthy of Machiavelli. On his return from exile in Spain in 1973 camouflaged snipers opened fire on the crowd at the airport and there were power struggles taking place within the various political factions; rumours of repression, and undisguised strife among a growing segment of the armed forces. So, finding himself in this highly volatile situation it was not unreasonable for Carlos to feel somewhat nervous.

Luckily for Carlos he was not alone. Perón had attended the show and then, following the tradition of the times, came 'backstage' to be introduced to the performers, who all lined up in a very straight line for their 'inspection'. Carlos recalls that to him Perón appeared very old, and looked very deteriorated at that time. He was obviously in severe pain and was walking with great difficulty. However, he clearly had not lost all his marbles. When he came to Carlo he said to him that he thought he was very like a woman. He too, touched him, and said, almost as if an echo of Michael York, is it true you don't have any bones? Carlos quickly disabused him, but in a much less flippant manner than he had done with York. At that time Carlos was known as, and his act was advertised as, *The boy with no bones!* Clearly the marketing worked.

Grace Kelly (Grace, Princess Consort of Monaco) - 1980

Apart from Peron the other person to make Carlos nervous was Grace Kelly, or Grace, Princess Consort of Monaco, to give her, her proper title.

Grace Kelly was a world-famous actress having come to fame by starring in films such as *High Noon* with Gary Cooper, winning an Oscar for Best Actress in *The Country Girl* as well as being the leading lady in several films for Director Alfred Hitchcock including *Rear Window* and *Dial M for Murder*. In 1955 Kelly headed the U.S. delegation at the Cannes Film Festival and was introduced to Prince Rainier III of Monaco. The following year they were married in what was considered to be the 'Wedding of the Century'. Prince Rainier was the sovereign of the principality of Monaco, a tiny city-state, located on the French Riviera, and reputed to be the wealthiest country in the world. It has no income tax, very low business tax and is a tax haven for a rich and powerful population consisting largely of millionaires and billionaires.

After her marriage Kelly made no more films but, despite leaving the world of theatre and films Kelly, as princess, continued to work actively for the arts helping to improve the arts institutions of Monaco, and eventually founding in 1964 the Princess Grace Foundation to support local artisans. In 1974, she and Prince Rainier, established the *International Circus Festival of Monte-Carlo*, known (in French) as *Festival International du Cirque de Monte-Carlo*. It was an annual festival held in late January or early February, and included the awarding of the *Clown d'Or* (Golden Clown) award as well as awards for other circus skills. The festival takes place in the Chapiteau (circus tent) de Fontvieille, which is a permanent venue was built specially for it and it was here in 1980 that Carlos first travelled to perform and to meet the illustrious princess, having of course been cheated out of a previous opportunity to perform at this event while with Circus Vargas.

After a breath-taking, and elegant performance on the Roman Rings, Carlos was invited to meet the Princess for canapés, in a marquee attached to the main venue. He was very nervous when she approached him and even more so when she spoke to him. She gently placed her hand on his forearm and said, *"Mr Medina, as a circus performer you are the most formidable contortionist in this current age, but in the air, you are the most graceful and beautiful ballet dancer I have ever seen."*

Despite her fame, wealth, and royal status, Carlos was impressed by the humility she showed, because, as he found previously when he met Elizabeth Taylor, she displayed no airs and graces, treated people as fellow human beings, and clearly did not consider them 'mere performers' cavorting solely for her pleasure. Carlos later recorded that going to Monte Carlo in 1980 to meet Princess Grace was one of the most wonderful moments in his life.

Part of Carlos' nervousness can no doubt be put down to her fame, but Carlos probably also felt indebted to her and in a way that it may be more difficult for us to comprehend. For Carlos, not only was she a film star, and a princess in her own right, but she was also an outspoken champion and patron of Circus Performers. She lifted them to the status of 'Artists'. As Carlos later remarked, "If it wasn't for Grace Kelly we circus performers would not have had a patron."

Before the establishment of the *International Circus Festival of Monte-Carlo,* circus performers were not considered to be Artists at all, but were treated somewhat contemptuously, and considered no better than street performers or buskers. Interestingly enough the word 'busk' comes from the old French 'busquer' meaning 'to seek, to prowl' and the Spanish 'buscar' 'to seek'. It is often considered that buskers are literally seeking fame and fortune. It was derived originally from a nautical term 'busk', "to cruise as a pirate". An older French form 'busquer' was often used to describe prostitutes and by 1841, it was being used in a figurative sense in reference to people living shiftless and peripatetic lives. Consequently 'busking' was often applied, in a derogatory way, to the activities of Romani Gypsies, presumably to the free spirit of their music, dancing and fortune telling. The etymology of these words shows that those who busked were considered to be engaging in an undesirable profession. For Carlos it was through the creation of the festival that Princess Grace was able to raise the status and improve the quality of life of all circus acts. She changed them from undesirable buskers, to respected creative artists in their own right!

While in Monte Carlo at the festival Carlos also met some of the most renowned clowns who were there to bask in Princess Grace's grace, through competing for the *Clown d'Or* (Golden Clown) award. Princess Grace was very good friends with Josep Andreu i Lasserre, best known as 'Charlie Rivel', an internationally known Spanish circus clown. She also knew Oleg Konstantinovich Popov - known as the "Sunshine clown". He was probably one of the most famous Russian clowns and circus artists in the world at that time. The following year, 1981, Popov was to win the so called "Oscar of the clown world": The Golden Clown award at the 8th International Circus Festival of Monte-Carlo. Another famous clown, Nicolai Poliakoff, more famously known as 'Coco the Clown' was of Russian descent and was a long time star of the *Bertram Mills Circus* here in England. He died in 1974 but his son Michael Polakovs performed in the USA under the same name as his father had used: 'Coco the Clown'.

Another star of the clowning world was Carletto "Charlie" Cairoli an Italian-English clown, impressionist and musician who died in February 1980 in Blackpool. Although Carlos never worked with him directly he did perform with his son, Charlie Cairoli Junior.

Carlos returned to Monte Carlo again in 1984. This time he went on holiday as a tourist, travelling with Billy Arata's wife, Margaret, who suggested the trip as a spur of the moment thing as her husband Billy was off visiting circuses somewhere else in Europe. Sadly, by this time, Princess Grace had gone. She died tragically in 1982 at the age of 52, after a car accident while travelling in the Côte d'Azur region in the South of France.

Princess Margaret – 1985

A few years after his wonderful visit to Monte Carlo, Carlos was scheduled to meet another member of the world's great Aristocracy, Princess Margaret. In 1985 the world was still reeling from the impact and fear of AIDS and HIV and it was to be another two years before the British Government launched a major public information campaign about the risks and dangers of AIDS. By the time that campaign was launched in, 1987, the World Health Organization had been notified of 43,880 cases of AIDS in 91 different countries. However, thankfully some time before this, socially conscious people had taken it upon themselves to act and were already trying to get the message out there; to try and disseminate some accurate and useful information about this tragic new killer disease, a disease that provoked hysterical reactions because of its link to, and association with, the Gay Community.

Here in England in, 1985, Carlos was asked to perform at an event being organized by an AIDS Charity in London, the *London Lighthouse*, which subsequently merged with the *Terrence Higgins Trust*. The president of the Charity at that time was Princess Margaret who was happy to use her royal position to help promote such a worthy cause. Carlos recalls the circumstances as follows:-

My circus director, Billy Arata, came to me and said "Medina if you don't mind, you are not going to work for 2 or 3 days, it is a charity for HIV positive. You are going to meet Princess Margaret." "Well," I said, "I am not interested in the money. Today I feel very healthy; but I don't know how I will feel tomorrow. I am gay myself too."

The event was being held in Battersea Park in South London and being staged by the *Robert Brothers Circus*. Unfortunately as it transpired Carlos was not able to meet the Princess as, after watching the show, which was running late, she had to depart straight away and instead of meeting the cast she was whisked off to another engagement. Carlos watched philosophically as her car drove past at gathering speed. He had not managed to meet her but at least he had been able to contribute to such a worthwhile cause and to help promote the normalization of homosexuality.

Chapter 12

SEXUALITY

Like most of us, if not us all, Carlos was seeking for love, affection and acceptance. Through his circus career Carlos had achieved not only acceptance but also a form of love; the love and adoration of the breath-gasping, thrill-seeking, ever appreciative applauding audience. But this was not enough for Carlos for he always knew he was different. He knew that something deep within him was not 'normal'. He never considered himself a gay man. Although he was born a man, looked like a man, and undoubtedly had the body of a man, in his heart, in his brain and in his mentality he often thought of himself as a woman.

His flamboyant manner, outrageous costumes and openly camp and flouncing manner were some of the ways that Carlos was able to manifest this 'feminine' side of himself throughout the course of his life. However, Carlos was not transgender, and certainly did not want to become a woman. Nor was he a cross-dresser either. He just had a strong sensitive, passive and feminine quality, that he felt the need to assert. His desire to wear outrageous, flamboyant and colourful clothes was done to startle and amaze his audience, to gain their applause and provide something uplifting for them. To give them a glimpse of another more wonderful and suffering-free world.

For Carlos, a long-time hero, and someone who was able to create that strange other-worldly effect was Liberace. He seemed to live in an ethereal and alternative reality, full of laugher, gaiety, glitter, wealth and extravagance. (Although of course we know the reality of his life was not at all like that.)

Carlos was performing with a circus in Mexico in 1974, shortly after branching out on his own, when the Circus Director's son, Alejandro, who was outrageously camp and sported a large flashy moustache, invited Carlos to go with him to nearby Tucson, Arizona to see Liberace perform. Carlos was delighted, even more so when Alejandro offered to pay. Even then, Liberace was incredibly popular and the tickets were 150 pesos each (about $15 US dollars) and this particular event had sold out weeks before. When they arrived, the venue was therefore completely full. This did not surprise Carlos, but what did, was the fact that the audience seemed to consist only of old ladies – Carlos could see no men anywhere! Alejandro, quickly explained to the puzzled looking Carlos that Liberace was 'gay', and therefore very attractive to the ladies. Carlos had never heard the word 'gay' before. In what must have been a very comical interlude Alejandro, in a rather ham-fisted way, tried to explain the term.

Alejandro: "You know who you are?"

"Yes," said Carlos proudly, "I am Robin Medina."

Alejandro: "No, no. You and I, we are different."

Carlos: "Yes. You are rich and I am poor."

The dialogue continued in that humorous form of miscommunication for some time until Alejandro was finally able to explain to Carlos slowly and carefully the full ramifications of the word 'gay'.

As he watched the show Carlos was very impressed by Liberace and his whole performance and also his cheeky style of banter. At one point a lady in the audience, who Liberace had brought up onto the stage, admired one of his beautiful and precious diamond rings that sparkled brightly under the floodlights. Quick as a flash Liberace quipped, "You pay to see that!" A retort which, as we saw in the meeting with Michael York, would not have been amiss coming out of Carlos' mouth. Carlos admired the sheer professionalism of Liberace and clearly Liberace had a powerful influence on Carlos' style and performance and probably helped him in some way to become even more outrageous and flamboyant than he had been previously.

Indeed, he henceforth began to manifest this extravagant, 'gay', showman side of himself even more as we have seen in the chapters above. We have also noted that much later in his career, *Robero's Circus* seemed happy to refer to him openly as, *"The Queen of the air"*. However, in a strange contradiction and application of double standards – an experience common to all gay people – although willing to play with double entendres in their programme, in reality the circus, like the majority of society, did not want its gay people to be active sexually. This applied even more so to those in charge of running the show, who not only had to oppress others but sometimes had to deny themselves. According to Carlos, the Circus Director of *Robero's Circus* at that time was a closet gay man himself and, as regards his sexual predilections Carlos, using the vernacular gay slang said of him, "He likes black pudding. I don't!" However, whatever the politics of it all, Carlos' experience was that on a human level, the majority of the people who lived, worked and inhabited the world of the circus saw you first and foremost as a performer; your private life was of no concern to them.

When he came to work in the UK, Carlos learned that the distinction between appearances and reality, the need to be able to play a role, and the willingness to fit in to society's mores, was much more rigorous and defined. Not only was homosexuality frowned upon, it was actually forbidden. In those days the circus considered itself as family entertainment, and families did not include gays! This is somewhat ironic considering Carlos' experience of 'traditional' heterosexual family life. A clause in the *Billy Smarts*, *Chipperfield* and *Gerry Cottle Circus*, contracts of the time, forbad gay performers from attending gay clubs, or gay bars and any such public display of homosexual behaviour was likewise frowned upon so it will be no surprise to learn that it was not until 1982 at the age of 32 that Carlos was first able to visit an openly gay establishment.

Carlos was never one to be subdued and was determined to always be able to assert his own individuality. He was particularly outraged by the fact that the *Gerry Cottle Circus* contract should adopt this ban on gay behaviour. Carlos was also a man who had a rather vicious side of himself that did not forget and more importantly did not forgive.

Carlos had first met Gerry Cottle in the early eighties, shortly after arriving in the UK when he was introduced to him by Billy Arata. Carlos was still rather unknown on the European Circus scene and Billy was trying to get Carlos some work with the *Gerry Cottle Circus*. At that first meeting, Gerry Cottle was very unpleasant indeed. He had apparently come to the irrational and erroneous conclusion that because he was so thin Carlos must have AIDS. Through fear of contracting the disease he refused to shake Carlos by the hand and instantly became very dismissive of Carlos and gave him a very wide berth indeed. Carlos was hurt but also incensed by this, as he had heard insalubrious rumours about Cottle himself.

From 1976 – 1985, the *Circus World Championships* were held in England and broadcast on the television each year. For the first few years they were broadcast by the BBC, with network specials being broadcast in America by both CBS and NBC. The format of the show was fairly simple. Each year the producers would select around five circus disciplines – such as trapeze or high wire - and have two or three acts compete against each other in each category. They also mixed in some additional acts, usually featuring animals, in order to present a balanced programme. The co-creator of the Championships was David Balding who subsequently worked for the *Chipperfields Circus* and the *Big Apple Circus* in New York, before setting up *Circus Flora* in America in 1986

The *Circus World Championships* had become a very famous event in the Circus calendar. Carlos - who by now was beginning to establish a reputation in UK circles as a highly skilled performer - had come to the Championships to see David Balding, as he was an old friend from his Circus Vargas days. Because of his connection to David, lots of rich and famous people were queuing up to congratulate Carlos after the show. Everyone wanted to see him and shake his hand. It was a very typical 'darling' and 'luvvy' theatrical event.

It so transpired that Gerry Cottle was also in the queue, and was now suddenly keen to congratulate Carlos on his successful career. However, having a long memory and still bearing the scar of that original smart, when he drew near Carlos said rather loudly to him, "You'd better not come near me. I'm gay. I'm queer." Much to Cottle's obvious embarrassment. Carlos always believed that people should be open and honest and despised hypocrisy. As we have seen, Carlos did eventually work for the *Gerry Cottle Circus* but by then it was no longer owned by its eponymous founder.

Carlos was slowly establishing himself with the *Hampsons Theatrical Agency* and Billy and Margaret had proven themselves to be good and true friends and Carlos continued to stay with them in the guest room of their house during circus engagements. On returning to Birmingham in December 1981, from a season in South Africa, Billy informed Carlos that he had been unable to secure any work for him over the Christmas period that year. However, he was quick to add that he had arranged for Carlos to perform a summer season in Macau. It also transpired that Billy and his wife were going to spend that Christmas in France as they were attending yet another famous Circus Competition. Although he knew he would not be made at all welcome, Carlos, at a complete loss, and not wishing to be left on his own, proposed, rather rashly, that he return to South America to visit his father in Columbia. Billy quickly pointed out that that there was no point in doing that, as it would be very expensive to travel all that way and he would have to spend nearly all his money on air fares. Carlos was very still very unhappy at the prospect of being left alone in Billy's house over Christmas, but there was little else he could do.

Billy was very good friends with a man who owned one of the few gay clubs in Birmingham at that time, and decided this would be a good opportunity for Carlos to explore that side of himself. The club in question was the *Jug*, situated on Albert Street, a popular and important venue of the time, and located underneath a very popular and famous India restaurant. The *Jug* was apparently an acronym of 'Just Us Guys' as it was initially a men-only club. However, after women were admitted the acronym was cleverly changed to 'Just Us Gays'. Its owner was something of a legend on the Birmingham Gay Scene; the very big hearted, flamboyant and colourful, Laurie Williams. It was here to the *Jug* in 1981, that Carlos first came to explore, and have his first taste of, the British Gay scene.

By that time in his life Carlos had had several sexual experiences but these had all been fleeting, one-off casual interactions. During his life Carlos had had sex with a total of only ten men. Although such promiscuity may seem shocking to heterosexual readers, to have had so few sexual encounters in one's life would be considered by many gay men to have lived a somewhat impoverished and sheltered life!

Given that his work involved constant travel and a tremendous level of disciple, Carlos never had a boyfriend. He believed that he was too selfish to share himself with anyone else, ascribing this to his strong personality and his need– often out of necessity – to always be a strong, independent and forceful character. This need for self-reliance was probably caused by his painful early experience when those who should have protected and looked after him failed to do so.

Carlos claimed then that he had never been in love, and considered himself to be someone who was always unlucky in love. Like the hero of many a dramatic love-story, the person that his heart yearned for did not want him, and likewise those who were attracted to him, unfortunately, he did not want. For Carlos the most important thing in life was the recognition and applause of an audience; that and good health.

It was crucial to him that he remain in excellent physical shape, as his body was his main source of livelihood so it will be no surprise that another factor that reined-in Carlos' appetite was his fear of becoming HIV positive. During the early years of the nineteen eighties, as the true terror of AIDS began to manifest itself, Carlos like many others at the time reeled back in fear from it, staggered by its scythe-like ability to kill so many, so quickly, and in such a horrific and painful way. Always a lover and admirer of beauty, Carlos was shocked to see so many beautiful young people dying needless and tragic deaths. It broke his heart to see beauty so ravaged. He therefore determined that if he ever contracted the disease he would contrive a way to kill himself rather than suffer the agony and torment that AIDS engendered. From that time onwards Carlos never had sex with another man.

Therefore, it was in this rather prophylactic mental state that Carlos first dipped his toes into the Birmingham gay scene. In those days, as he was still an active performer and needed to stay in excellent physical shape Carlos drank only Coca Cola. He recalls being met at the door of the *Jug* by Laurie Williams in a flamboyant and outrageous way. At that time Laurie was renowned for greeting everyone with the Birmingham expression 'babs'. He led Carlos downstairs into the glittering club, and procured for him a very large glass of Coca Cola. Carlos recalls the glass seemed to be about twelve inches tall and it took him about three hours to drink it, taking small sips so as not to offend his host.

Laurie clearly took a shine to Carlos and no doubt enjoyed his cheeky banter and equally flamboyant and outrageous behaviour. During the course of the evening Carlos told Laurie his disappointment at being left alone over Xmas in the Hampson's house. Although he was grateful for a roof over his head, for Carlos the tragedy of it all was that it meant he would have to forgo his usual Christmas indulgence of filling the house with flowers and eating traditional Italian Panettone. On hearing this outrageous news, Laurie immediately invited Carlos to stay with him and his partner, Lionel Strawbridge, over the duration of the Christmas holiday. Far be it from Laurie that another human should have to suffer this level of deprivation. Carlos was delighted by this offer and quickly and gratefully accepted, and from that time forth Laurie and Carlos became firm friends and Carlos visited the *Jug* whenever he was based for any length of time in Birmingham.

Sometime later an old American friend of Carlos, whose circus was visiting Birmingham and performing at the Alexandra Stadium, invited Carlos to perform in one of their shows. It just so happened that Laurie Williams also caught that same show. When they met in the *Jug* a few days later, Laurie in characteristic camp fashion said to him, "Babs I never knew you were such a strong girl in the air like that."

In the early eighties there were very few gay bars in Birmingham the other main one being the *Jester*, located underneath Scala House on Holloway Circus. At the *Jug*, Carlos had met and befriended two old queens, Harry and Roy, who were long time sexual partners. They told Carlos that he was so outrageous that they wanted to take him to the *Jester*. At that time David

Brown was the owner of the *Jester* and, always happy to oblige, Carlos readily accompanied Harry and Roy to visit this much vaunted venue.

When he first arrived Carlos was rather taken aback as David Brown said to him; "I have heard about you Caracas maracas" and flounced off. Carlos turned to his friends in shocked surprised and said, "He has insulted me, he called me, 'Caracas maracas'". Harry and Roy, laughed and applauded like overexcited school girls and were delighted. They informed Carlos that to be insulted by David Brown was a clear sign that he likes you. They went on to explain that the people David really likes he 'takes the piss out of' and if he doesn't like someone, he cuts them off cold, and won't say a word to them. So here too, Carlos had been quickly welcomed into the fold, and had found yet another refuge he could visit for company, companionship and to exercise his constant desire to perform.

In time, Carlos came to learn that the *Victoria Bar* at the back of the *Alexandra Theatre* also welcomed gays, although it was not strictly a gay bar. Most pubs in the City were legally obliged to close by one in the morning but when the Victoria had events and provided food, they were able to stay open later and Carlos occasionally found himself there, enjoying the rowdy party atmosphere well into the early morning hours.

For Carlos, like many gay men of the time, and many still now, the Gay Scene was not really a place to find sex, although a lot did use it that way. It was more of an opportunity to meet with like-minded individuals, build friendships, have a social life and develop warm, friendly, human relationships without the need to wear the mask of normality that 'straight' society demanded. Looking back, Carlos was to reflect that in those early days of gay emancipation the old fashioned bars were homosexual clubs run for homosexual gentleman with equality and dignity. Not like today's bars where the emphasis seems to be solely on sex and an over infatuation and obsession with looks and size!

Chapter 13

COLOGNE 27th OCTOBER 1989

In 1989 Carlos was in Cologne performing for the Circus Carl Busch a German circus, which had been founded by the original Carl Busch in Nuremberg in 1891, and handed down through various family members over several generations. On the continent it was much more common for a circus to be based in a city for several months each year than here in the UK, and Carlos had been contracted to appear with Circus Carl Busch in Cologne for a season lasting some two-and-a-half months.

Cologne is Germany's fourth-largest city it is also very beautiful, straddling both sides of the magnificent river Rhine which flows slowly and majestically past, on its hundred-mile journey to the North Sea. The city is dominated by the catholic Cathedral, a massive building which took over seven centuries to complete and whose twin steeple towers, embellished with ornate carvings, rise up into the air to a height of some 157 metres (515 feet) dwarfing the houses and the city below. It is as if the inhabitants not only wanted to glorify God with this edifice but also to almost try and reach up and touch him too. The external walls of the building are made of stone, a stone stained black by the sulphur content in the air, due to the time when the inhabitants of the city burned coal in their fires. The whole structure, dominating the city as it does exudes an ominous, foreboding and medieval atmosphere.

Carlos discovered that in Germany, as in America, everything had to be spectacular: not only their cathedrals but even their circuses. Whether they were trying to compete with the spires of the cathedral or whether they were just being extravagant is unclear, but what was very clear was that even to Carlos, who by this time had performed in venues all over the world, the sheer height of the *Circus Carl Busch* Big Top was, to say the least, somewhat daunting.

In Cologne the month of October is characterized by rapidly falling temperatures, with daily highs decreasing from 18°C to 13°C. By the 27th of the month the weather would certainly be cool, if not decidedly cold. On that Friday afternoon as he was leaving his caravan to cross into the ring, Carlos felt a cold chill rise up his spine. He was disturbed. Whether it was to do with the foreboding atmosphere generated by the blackness of the Cathedral, or whether it was a message, an intercession, arising from the prophetic wisdom of his devoutly catholic great-grandmother, whose words the young Carlos thought seemed to shake heaven and earth, or whether or not it was just the niggling daily doubts about the meaning or purpose of life which hit us all from time to time, Carlos was agitated and concerned.

Instead of crossing into the Big Top he decided to go for a walk to see if he could allay his concerns. As he wandered the cold and still deserted streets, around the circus location, he resolved to seek reassurance. Through racking his brains Carlos had come to the conclusion that his main concern and anxiety was to do with his rigging, and he determined that he wanted to check it.

Aerial rigging is the term given to the process of setting up the complex equipment which is used to hold up the trapeze, and the Roman Rings and those 'invisible' wires that make humans appear to fly through the air. It is a highly specialised field and its proper execution is essential in order to insure the safety of the artists and the audience. It is normally carried out by specialty fabricators, professional riggers, or professional aerial artists. However, although it was the preserve of specialist, it did not then have all the rigours, regulations and legal requirements that are now in place. The following year 1990, thanks to the EU, sweeping new Health and Safety regulations came into being, and the sanctity of life came to be valued more than profit. Safety nets were made compulsory and additional chains and backup systems became the norm. That same raft of regulations also ensured that all people who worked in dangerous or potentially life-threatening occupations were required to obtain full life and medical insurance.

As a professional aerial artist, Carlos had been trained to set up and test his own rigging, and the sprained ankles and legs that he sustained over the years from minor falls, had driven home to him the necessity of ensuring that the whole rig was always as safe and sound as he could possibly make it.

The rigging was generally installed while the Big Top was still on the ground. As Carlos did his own rigging, he spent many an hour crawling under the heavy canvas before it was raised up in to position. This was not a job for glitz and glamour; banished were the sequins and the flamboyant feather hats, here he wore dungarees and sweated and strained like the other labourers who were struggling to ensure that all the wires, cables and equipment were in place prior to their final exertions as the Big Top was raised. Carlos would assemble his equipment, checking it thoroughly, then bolt it onto the roof beams before finally screwing it into place and tightening it, as tight as his not-inconsiderable strength could ensure.

Carlos, acting on his intuition and his resolution arrived back from his fretful walk and went straight to see the Circus Director, Carl Busch and told him that he needed to check his rigging. Although sympathetic to his concerns, Mr Busch said that that would not be possible. He explained that in Germany, after the big top has gone up, people are not allowed to go near the rigging in case they fall and kill themselves. This was not a good enough explanation, and Carlos insisted that he needed to check the rigging immediately. Adamant though he was, the answer was still no.

Concerned, but not thwarted, Carlos approached the Director's son, Kala, who he had struck up a mutual friendship with and asked him if he would intervene and ask his father a favour. He explained to Kala that he had real concerns that there was some kind of problem with his rigging. Carlos pleaded with Kala to go to his father and persuade him to let him check his rigging. Kala promised nothing, but said he was certainly willing to go and talk to his father. This was mid-afternoon. Eventually by five o'clock Mr Busch came back. He had obviously been persuaded by his son, and informed Carlos that, as it was only an hour before the performance, he could not arrange it today, but that Carlos could check the rigging as thoroughly as he wanted the following day.

Always the pragmatist, Carlos accepted the decision and went to prepare himself for the evening's show. That night at a height of forty feet above the ground and executing his amazing spinning routine the rigging gave way and Carlos, to the dismay and gasps of the watching audience, fell to the ground like a sparkling but featherless Icarus.

Panic ensued. There was no safety net and Carlos had landed with a loud thud on the sawdust strewn boards of the main circus ring. Luckily for him his years of training instinctively kicked in. As a boy almost one of the first things his circus family had taught him was how to fall correctly. Carlos was still conscious but had broken his left leg. With legendary German efficiency he was rushed to the local hospital where they began to insert metal pins into his bones, and placed him in traction, to ensure his leg would heal properly.

The Director and his son, and indeed his whole family, were beside themselves with remorse and visited Carlos every day over the ensuing weeks. Carlos remained very positive and stoical about the whole experience, and reassured himself that in Europe Circus Directors really cared for the artists they engaged, and also for the quality and professionalism of their performance, contrasting this with his experience in South America where they did not. Carlos reflected that if this accident had happened in South America, he would probably have ended up in a wheelchair, or worse, have died. So, oddly enough, he took some comfort and indeed was even grateful that such a serious accident took place, as it did, here in Europe. Carlos had also been very lucky that he was so fit and agile, as, by virtue of his training, his reactions and his muscular body, he had been able to absorb a lot of the impact of the fall. His hard-won flexibility and strength had helped to reduce the potentially catastrophic effect of the landing.

It was to take Carlos a year and three months to fully recover from this fall, a fall that marked the end of his circus career. He was 38 years old.

As soon as they heard the news, Billy Arata and Margaret determined that Carlos should be moved from the hospital in Cologne to one in England. After all, Carlos did not speak any German, and had no real friends or contacts there. Billy immediately made arrangements for Carlos to be admitted to Woodlands Hospital (now the Royal Orthopaedic Hospital) on the Bristol Road, in Birmingham. Not only would he be near to the Hampsons, but this hospital was famous for its great technical and academic advances, and for employing many famous Doctors who helped advance orthopaedic surgery. This was clearly the best place for Carlos; to be surrounded by exceptional surgeons who specialized in dealing with leg trauma. Billy and Margaret took great care of all the necessary details, and a very bruised but grateful Carlos soon began to realize that to him, they were like the family he never had.

Thanks to the high level of care that Carlos received the hospital were soon able to remove the metal pins used to hold the bones in place - pins he still has in his possession to this day - and to start him on the physiotherapy guided road to recovery. The main down side of all this time away from his craft was that he began to put on a lot of weight, going from the sylph-like figure of six and a half stone to nearly double the size – twelve and a half stone.

No longer having a profession to pursue when he left hospital, Margaret and Billy, insisted that he continue to stay in their home. Billy also helped him negotiate the UK's benefits system. Carlos was legally registered as living in this country and had been since 1982, and was therefore eligible for disability allowance and unemployment benefit. As Billy said to him, "You were one of the greatest circus aerial contortionists in the world; I do not want to see you on the street". Not only had Billy and Margaret succeeded in helping him to recover from the most serious fall in his career, but they had also helped him get established in Birmingham and to begin to build a new way of life.

Chapter 14

A NEW LIFE – THE GAY SCENE REVISITED

By Christmas 1990 Carlos had finally completed the whole slow, painful, process of healing his broken bones, and twisted sinews, and learned how to walk again. Although he had put on a lot of weight he was still very supple through years spent practicing his craft, but his circus career was definitely over. No longer would he stand arrayed in white and covered in sequins dazzling in the spotlight, nor hear the loud shouts of admiration and applause that he so craved for and so loved. Now that he could walk once more, he also had to learn how to live again.

Billy and Margaret had been incredibly supportive throughout his whole ordeal helping him through his slow recovery and providing him with all his material needs, but there was still something missing. It now seemed sensible, that as he had such stalwart friends as the Hampsons who were based in Birmingham, that Carlos too, should no longer consider Birmingham just as a working base, but that he should settle here, call it his home, and make his new life in the city.

At the age of forty, Carlos found himself unemployed for the first time in his life. He had no real transferable skills that he could use in another occupation and his body, although recovered to a very great degree, had suffered a tremendous trauma, to such an extent that he was officially considered to be disabled and would have to learn to live off state disability benefits for the rest of his life.

For most of us the random events that seem to make up our life propel us forward so quickly and so totally that we seldom have cause to question them. We create a self, which we believe is constant and real, and relate to the world as if this was axiomatically true. We have a history and behave on a daily basis from the moment we get up as if we are going to have an eternal future too. Very few people step back and reflect on their life, what they have done, what they could do, why they did what they did. Some ask searing questions and speculate about why we are here and if there is a purpose to it all, but very few use it to determine their actions on a daily basis.

Carlos had been given this somewhat dubious opportunity; an opportunity few might relish but it's true that often a near death experience has the effect of making life seem all the more important and precious. During his time in the hospital and the long, long, days he spent on his back staring up at the ceiling, unable to move, Carlos had had time to reflect on his life:

Knowing he was no longer able to work or earn a living he reflected on the fact that money does not always buy love or happiness. He knew from the many that he had met, that millionaires are not always very happy people. He reflected on the life of Liberace and that, despite the fact that he had all that money, and all those wonderful sparkling diamonds, he still had to pay rent-boys for sex and affection.

Carlos reflected that he was still alive and healthy and had once again the use of his legs. He therefore concluded that health and happiness were important to him in his life. He rejoiced in the simple fact that he was still alive and healthy. He reflected too that he knew many blind people who could not see, and many disabled people who could not walk, but who were also perfectly happy with their lot. He reflected on how important kindness was. He reflected on the way that someone as rich and famous as Elizabeth Taylor had treated him and his circus family, reflected on the dignity, simplicity, kindness and humility that both she and Richard Burton had shown towards them. They were human too and had not been influenced by either their wealth or their fame to think they were beyond the hand of death. He reflected also on the fact that during his life he had achieved a lot. The kind admiring words of Princess Grace, a lady who had seen the best in the world perform before her, and yet still saw fit to compliment Carlos in such an effusive and moving way. Despite all that had happened to him Carlos was truly grateful for what he had, and was now determined to make the best of what was yet to come. It was with this positive philosophical scaffolding in place that Carlos ventured out yet again to join the rest of humanity on the often painful and disappointing journey of life.

Having been based in Birmingham before, while he was still travelling and performing and living in his caravan, Carlos had made many friends on the Gay Scene and it seemed an important and helpful first step to renew those acquaintances. At least there he would be able to fit in and learn how to socialize again. In those days many of the gay bars and clubs still adhered to the philosophy promoted by Laurie Williams of being places where homosexual men and women could come together with equality and dignity: where like-minded companions could be found and strong life-long friendships could be formed. The Gay Community is, by and large, a caring community, and the people who make it up are concerned, thoughtful and generous, having had to battle against the norms of society in order to establish a sense of independent identity for themselves. Carlos, therefore, was very quickly and enthusiastically welcomed back into the bosom of the Gay Scene.

Laurie Williams and *The Jug* were still there, although strangely relocated to a rather run-down area of the City, known as the Jewellery Quarter. There were many who thought that Laurie was not a very savvy businessman, and the various business ventures he engaged in seemed often to exist in a kind of hand to mouth sort of way. However, *Nightingales*, and *The Jester*, were still going strong, and new venues like *Missing* and *The Village* had begun to spring up in and around Hurst Street, in what was eventually to become the Gay Quarter of Birmingham. Laurie Williams eventually moved into Hurst Street too, opening a new venue called *Laurie's International Club*, in time for Birmingham's first Gay Pride 1997. This venue shocked many people by having clear glass windows which opened onto the street, enabling those who passed by to look through the glass and see real live gays drinking and talking! It later became '*Angels Bar*' and has morphed through several other transformations.

Although no longer able to 'perform' in the circus sense of the word, Carlos soon found that the Gay Scene was really just another type of circus. It afforded him an opportunity to perform, to be daring, to shock people with his outrageous behaviour, and to say things that other people would be afraid to utter. Before long he had established himself as the life and soul of the party, the true Belle of the Ball. He literally was the Belle of the Gay Ball in 2003 where he appears on the poster along with others advertising the event, decked out in an elaborate glittering and sparkling pink costume with an even more extravagant pink feather hat!

Carlos became famous or infamous on the scene for his rather bizarre catch phrase or catchword – 'really!' Carlos uttered it as a long drown out phrase in a loud and commanding voice, pronouncing it as if it were a question: "Reeeee-lly?"

He was also still surprisingly supple enough to be able to kick his leg straight up into the air past his head. With these simple skills, and his warm, generous and witty personality Carlos began to build his new life, a rather humble and much more simple life, compared to what he once had, but one which enabled him to live from day to day.

Carlos was fêted by his many friends on the scene: invited out for meals, taken to events, to theatre performances, to musical recitals, and even to see other circus performances. Carlos still had many friends in the circus world too, and they often invited him to see them perform when they were in the country. However, the main down-side of all this 'gay' new life was that because Carlos was no longer required to keep up the discipline of remaining in a state of perfect physical fitness in order to discharge his profession, he began to drink alcohol. It seems somewhat ironic to think that it was in a City like Birmingham where the Cadbury family, great leaders of the Quaker temperance movement, not only lived and thrived, but also set up their huge Chocolate Factory to help people deal with and replace their alcohol addiction, that Carlos finally came face to face with the demon drink. Not only did he come face to face with it he totally embraced it, and kissed it fully and longingly on the lips.

Alcohol is a strange beast indeed. In the early stages of its consumption – after one quickly ignores the unpleasant taste – it produces a warm, pleasant and satisfying effect. Soon one feels relaxed and the normal inhibitors on our emotions seem to drop away and we feel energetic, expansive and capable of anything. We suddenly seem awash with ideas, and feelings that we would normally repress or deny are given full reign and we become euphoric. Our feelings of love for our brother man are suddenly magnified and those we are drinking with, not only provide us with enjoyable, and entertaining company but also seem to understand us truly and deeply in a manner that no one has ever been able to understand us before. Given all this, it is not surprising that one wants to regain this enjoyable state again and again. However, we all know that following this state of temporary elation there is the down side, the state that over indulgence brings. The sickness, the inability to control one's muscles, the sometimes hidden violence and aggression that emerges, and the dreadful and painful hangovers when one's head and body seem to be beating one mercilessly with aches and pains and loud unending clashing of cymbals. So, for Carlos, as for so many others, the Gay Scene brought friendship, warmth and even elation, but at a price!

Billy and Margaret were open minded people engaged in a very fluid, flamboyant and possibly morally lax world, which entertainment so often seems to be. Even though they were married they both had the freedom to pursue their own private affairs. During the time Carlos stayed with them Billy was often abroad for long periods of time pursuing other circus performers and searching out acts to add to their portfolio. On these occasions Margaret entertained her lover, a Romanian called Victor Patresco. One day while Carlos was sitting reading in his room, Patresco, burst in, stark naked, and attempted to seduce him. Carlos was shocked and outraged and valiantly fought him off eventually managing to smack him across the face with a glass, which luckily did not shatter. In a state of total bewilderment and distress Carlos called two supportive friends from the gay scene, Kevin and Paul, who immediately and willingly came to his rescue.

Kevin and Paul had always been rather suspicious of Margaret and her lover and were already outraged by the fact that she and Billy had spent their life taking 10% of the money Carlos had earned while he worked for the circus and, in their opinion, "…treating him like shit" so they quickly and happily helped him to move out. They found Carlos a flat in Poplar Road in Bearwood, a district of Birmingham, just off the Hagley Road, the main artery into and out of the city. Carlos moved into this flat in 1993. It was to be the first of several flats he lived in, in various parts of Birmingham including, Quinton, Moseley, and Aston before finally settling into a newly-build, modern, ground-floor flat in Attwood Green.

Since his first return to it in 1990 the gay scene had changed. After the Sexual Offences Bill was passed in 1967, legalizing aspects of gay relationships for consenting adults over the age of 21, Britain slowly began to change its view of homosexual men and women and a new sense of openness and tolerance began to prevail. More and more people began to 'come out' publicly declaring their openly homosexual feelings towards others of the same sex. Popular television shows like East Enders showed the first homosexual kiss in the early hours of the evening and entertainers who had previously been hidden in the closet were now out and in your face. The world had become a gayer place. As more and more young men and women came out at an earlier and earlier age the Gay Scene became, once again like New York in the 80's, the party scene, and drinks, drugs and promiscuous sex became rampant once again. The bad old fearful days when life was threatened by the horrific killer AIDS seemed to have been very quickly forgotten.

For Carlos this change did not always seem be for the best. He had always been attracted to beauty, to good looking people with a pretty face, but more importantly, for him, what mattered most was the inner beauty of a person. For Carlos there is no sense in being the most beautiful person in the world if you are ugly inside and have a horrible personality. The Gay Scene which had originally been a refuge for troubled persecuted and misunderstood men and women seeking to find some rational way to make sense of their feelings, gave way to an infatuation with beauty and, good looks for good looks sake. 'Eye-candy' had become the new goal, and people were judged on how sexy and physically attractive they looked, regardless of how they behaved. The qualities of greed, bitchiness and backbiting exemplified in shows like Big Brother gave the nation a new model of moral behaviour that was easy to follow, and required no skill or ability to emulate. Carlos thought back to his visit to see Liberace perform and of Liberace's quick and rapier-like wit which was considered, cheeky and professional (and accomplished after a lot of practice and hard work) - totally unlike the undignified, and rude behaviour that began to manifest as 'cool' on the now transformed gay scene. Another manifestation of this changing world, and something that Carlos considered even more bizarre, was the open obsession and infatuation with size!

Clearly not everyone on the gay scene was this shallow, and even those who fell under the spell and the lure of the 'get famous quick' culture which pervaded the popular media, soon learned how vacuous and unrewarding it was.

Carlos continued to visit a variety of bars and coffee houses, meeting up with friends and acquaintances, and building and deepening his relationships. For a while he was happy to help his friend Trevor, who was struggling to set up a new business on the scene. Carlos, despite his 'broken' body which made it difficult for him to do any sustained or prolonged work, was a very fastidious cleaner. He took great pride in his work and was methodical and meticulous with any task he was given. Trevor, who was a kind and generous man, also knew that Carlos was prone to bouts of depression, loneliness and sometimes even self-pity and had taken him on to help Carlos avoid the pain of loneliness. Trevor was happy to give Carlos something to occupy him and also happy too to repay him by buying him a few drinks at the end of the day. The fact that Carlos turned out to be a first-class cleaner was a clear bonus.

Loneliness is a common problem on the gay scene and in most bars on most nights one can see lonely men and women seeking love and acceptance. Trevor could not bear to see Carlos sad and introduced Carlos to his family, invited him round for meals. Both Trevor's mother and father knew and cared for Carlos too. Sometimes when life got too much for him and Carlos broke down and cried Trevor would say to him: 'You know my family. You know the number of my mother and father. Call them up. You can phone my mother anytime you want, she loves speaking to you!'

Thus, with many dear and kind friends anxious to look after him Carlos continued to live out his new life. However, out of the blue he was to receive an odd but pleasant bonus from the life he thought he had left so very far behind.

Chapter 15

DAME BARBARA CARTLAND: JOURNEY TO A BIOGRAPHY

Dame Barbara Cartland, was born Mary Barbara Hamilton Cartland at 31 Augustus Road, Edgbaston, Birmingham, England on 9th July 1901. Her father was an army officer and she enjoyed a relatively comfortable middle-class existence. She began to write fairly early in her life and by the age of twenty-one had published her first novel, *Jigsaw* (1922), which became a best seller. After such an early success she went on to become one of the most prolific and commercially successful authors of the 20th century. By the time of her death in May 2000 she had written over 700 novels which had been translated into thirty-six different languages!

Barbara Cartland married Alexander George McCorquodale, a British Army officer from Scotland and enjoyed visiting Scotland developing a particular fondness for Caithness Sound on the north east side of the Country, where she often went to visit good friends of hers who owned Dunbeath Castle.

In 1990, after deciding to make Birmingham his home for good, we have seen that Carlos began to spend more and more time on the Gay Scene; learning to drink and making new friends in a new world. Two such friends were Kevin Fletcher and Paul Cox who, incidentally, were both dentists. Kevin and Paul, were a gay couple, and enjoyed Carlos' outrageous approach to life and took great delighted in hearing him recount tales of his meetings with the rich and famous and his death-defying adventures as an aerial contortionist.

It eventually transpired that Kevin and Paul also knew Barbara Cartland very well indeed. They had come to know her through a mutual friend of theirs who lived in Scotland. It appeared that while visiting their friend they would often end up visiting the great Dame when she was staying at Dunbeath Castle. They also often went to visit her in her beloved home at Camfield Place in Hertfordshire too.

One night in *The Jester*, Kevin and Paul told Carlos that they had mentioned him to the great Dame. The story goes that during one of their visits to Camfield they had told her of a friend of theirs called 'Carlos'. Intrigued by the name, and in a romantic fit of fancy, she imagined that all her heroes were called Carlos, and that all Latin men were gigolos. In this vein of romantic intoxication, she demanded to know if he was Italian or Portuguese or even Spanish. Somewhat archly Kevin and Paul triumphantly replied that Carlos was not only a native of Venezuela but also a circus performer. But not just that, a famous circus performer, a contortionist who executed daring feats of bravado high up on the Roman Rings. They succeeded in fascinating the great lady even more, and after hearing more tales about this exotic-sounding 'Carlos', Dame Barbara demanded to meet him. It appears that she had somehow alighted on the idea that she would like to write his biography. Unaware of this hidden agenda, Carlos was more than happy to accept when sometime in 1997, Kevin and Paul invited him to join them on a visit to the Scottish Highlands.

Kevin & Paul were very pleased with this outcome and drove Carlos to Scotland happily paying for everything, including the very beautiful countryside hotel in which they stayed. Carlos' first sight of the great lady was to see her standing in the middle of a river fishing for trout. She cut a rather bizarre figure, in the somewhat wild and craggy river bed, for she was attired in her normal pink ball gown, the bottom of which was tucked carefully into her green wellington boots. After meeting her in person for the first time, Carlos determined that she was a very graceful, but extremely eccentric lady, who liked to drink Gin and Tonic and, from time to time, Pink Champagne too.

That evening Dame Barbara invited Carlos, Kevin and Paul to dine with her at Dunbeath Castle where Carlos regaled them with tales for his time in the circus, and Barbara Cartland asked him many, many questions before telling them about her forthcoming novel and ranging over a great number of other topics in all of which, certainly as far as Carlos could determine, she seemed to be very well informed.

Carlos saw the great Dame in Scotland a second time shortly after that. Kevin and Paul were taking Carlos on a tour of Scotland but mostly with the intention of visiting John O'Groats. However they more than happily made a sweeping detour to Dunbeath Castle when they heard the great lady was in residence. Once again Carlos was made very welcome and over dinner few people were able to get a word in edgewise while Carlos and Barbara held the floor with their witty and sparkling banter.

A short time after this the great lady invited the trio to visit her in her English home. Since 1950, Dame Barbara had lived and worked at her beloved Camfield Place, the former home of Beatrix Potter. Camfield Place is a ten-bedroom mansion set in 400 acres of farmland and woods in Essendon near Hatfield, Hertfordshire, and it was here, to this ornately and lavishly furnished abode that Carlos travelled to meet her for the third time.

Carlos could not help but be impressed when Kevin and Paul's car turned off the narrow country road, and glided slowly through the imposing yellow brick pillars, topped off with replica Greek urns, that supported the delicately ornate wrought-iron gate at the entrance to this private estate. As they drove slowly down the curved drive he caught his first glimpse of the regal splendour of the ivy covered mansion.

The inside of the house was the definition of opulence and flamboyance, decorated throughout in pinks or pale reds, and with countless vases of extravagant pink flower arrangements everywhere. Carlos, with his precocious, florid and cheeky personality was more than a match for the formal Dame, and when they met sparks seemed to fly as they exchanged witty and teasing banter with each other.

Carlos and Dame Barbara Cartland and friend - Camfield Place

Barbara Cartland, like Carlos, was the epitome of flamboyance and extravagance. She liked the throw lavish dinner parties. On his first visit to Camfield Place he had been invited to lunch, during which time several glasses of gin and tonic were consumed, followed by several more glasses of Pink Champagne. During all this the Dame comported herself so regally that Carlos was left with an indelible image of her. He remembers coming away with the distinct impression, and the full and complete reinforcement of previous impressions, that she was indeed a proper English lady.

By now Carlos was aware that, even though the topic was only approached obliquely, this initial visit to Hatfield had been a sounding-out exercise for a potential biography. He was also to learn that once Dame Cartland had determined to do something, she was not easily dissuaded from it. She asked him many, many questions about his life, and his work with the circus, and the other famous people that he had met. After the meeting Dame Cartland announced that she was resolved to start work on the book straight away. Although intoxicated by the lavish attention - and no doubt a little by the Champagne too - Carlos was still harbouring some unspoken reservation.

Carlos met her again in December 1999 and on that occasion he brought her chocolates. She responded on the 14th December by sending him a short but polite thank you note, displaying the elaborate crest and bright red ink of the Camfield Place address, and a flamboyant pink scrawl of a signature. She was apparently known for her generous habits, and was often reported as having said that "one could never say thank you enough", which she did in abundance in this little note, stating, "Thank you again a thousand times."

When he visited her on 8th March 2000, Carlos took her some pink candles. In customary fashion she responded later that day with a short note filled with a profusion of thank yous and best wishes. During this visit the discussion quickly and overtly turned to the topic of her writing a book about Carlos, whether through an awareness that time was running out for her, or because she was impatient to be started on a new project we do not know. Strangely, for a man who had spent most of his life seeking the limelight, Carlos' reaction was negative. He thought, *"No. No. No. Who would want to buy a book about me: about all my sad and bad memories?"* In a moment of startling and honest self-knowledge he contemplated his being, and concluded, *"I am a very lonely, emotional, and sentimental old man, who would want to read about me?"* He felt ashamed and unworthy of this incredibly generous offer of immortality from such a famous and respected novelist, and so he refused, and Barbara Cartland was denied the opportunity to ever write anything about him.

During previous visits to Camfield Place, Carlos had also met her sons, Ian and Glen McCorquodale, from her second marriage. (Barbara Cartland's married name was Barbara McCorquodale, but she used her maiden name Cartland in all her books.) During April, her health began to deteriorate and Kevin and Paul informed Carlos that she was not very well, but that she was as determined as ever to write his biography. They also informed Carlos that if he was willing to go ahead with the book she would ask her son, Ian, to carry on with it. Carlos remained resolute in his refusal.

During May her health continued to fail and Carlos sent her a get well card to which, on the 17th May 2000, her secretary kindly replied thanking Carlos for his good wishes. Sadly that was the end of the matter, for Barbara Cartland passed away on May 21st, 2000, aged 98.

On the following day, the 22nd May 2000, the Daily Telegraph published an obituary which contains this wonderful image of the great lady who was so keen to add Carlos to her list of literary achievements:

"In her later years, she cut an unmistakeable figure in a froth of pink ball gown with extravagant, almost clown-like, make-up - her cheeks pulled back with sadly visible bits of sticking plaster. This facade of pancake and tulle, however, concealed an iron constitution, a steely determination, and a mind which, though often contrary and in an eccentric orbit of its own, was seldom less than razor sharp. She was a formidable fairy queen."

Chapter 16

FIRST ENCOUNTER
CARLOS: MORE SWINGS THAN
ROUNDABOUTS

It was an unexceptional bar on an unexceptional day and I was expecting the unexceptional. Like most bars of its kind, it was rather cramped and dark. The brown painted walls helped hide the nicotine stains from the clouds of deadly smoke that rose to the ceiling, and the dark brown leather sofas did the same. It was just after five pm and a handful of people had gathered, popping in from work for that quick pint before heading off home. The bar was fairly quiet although there was a gentle background murmur as conversations rose and died. The usual polite weather-oriented exchange between strangers dwindled and fell to silence, before rising again in a flurry of hope. Suddenly, a commotion in the street shattered the domestic stillness of the bar. People looked around startled. The large, roof-to-floor window which overlooked the pavement became the focus for many eyes, including my own. It was winter and the street outside was dark. The few street lights that were within sight gave the appearance of casting more shadows than light. Nothing could be seen.

The noise seemed to be approaching and was getting nearer and nearer until at last the door swung dramatically open. A diminutive, stocky gentleman stood framed in the doorway and seemed to pause for theatrical effect before commandingly flouncing into the bar. He was dressed in a thick Abercrombie-style overcoat, with a scarf thrown apparently carelessly about his neck, and armed with a full length umbrella.

His thick black hair bounced and waved over his head as his large, square, well-lived face, seemed to sparkle with mischief and life. He stood drinking in the effect his arrival had provoked. His eyes peered cheekily over his glasses as suddenly and apropos of nothing, he announced boldly, in a thick foreign accent, to the assembled onlookers...

"REEEEEE-LY!"

The unexpected, unanticipated and unpredictably exceptional, had arrived.

I was sitting in a quiet corner at the back of the bar which, as it consisting of only one room, was therefore completely visible by all to all, at all times. I watched as the stranger made his way to the bar. He was obviously well known here and many who sat on the high bar stools and had previously been sitting in silence suddenly seemed to perk up and gratefully greeted him by name - 'Carlos'. It was clear that he was the life and soul of the party as well as being the outrageous trickster, addressing someone very loudly and provocatively as, "My little Chicken". In very swift succession someone moved to provide him with a seat while someone else bought him a drink. Carlos had clearly arrived.

I sat quietly in the shadows, slowly supping my pint and happy to enjoy my own company and observe the rituals in this unfamiliar environment. Over the space of an hour or two, I witnessed, several others buy drinks for the mysterious but charismatic 'Carlos' too. He was clearly popular. As the ebb and flow of customers progressed throughout the evening with new people arriving to replace those who had left, all of them engaged in the ritual of greeting Carlos with obvious pleasure. Many were blessed with large and extravagant mouth to mouth kisses, provided apparently, more for the watching audience than those being kissed. The volume level had increased since his arrival and the growing crowd around him seemed to be declaiming their lines as if in some macabre pantomime. But this was real life!

After a few hours I decided it was time to go, so I got up and left quietly and unnoticed but with a very strong impression of this striking character embedded deeply into my brain.

The year was probably 1997 and at that time I was doing a lot of travelling in relation to my work, returning to Birmingham in between trips so there may well have been sometime between this first encounter, and my seeing him again. Eventually, the Birmingham Gay Scene being rather small, it was probable that we would run into each other again.

Due to my frequent travel away from the City, my visits to gay haunts were sporadic and spontaneous and when I did go out I tended to visit a handful of different bars depending on my mood: *Missing, The Village, Nightingales* and even occasionally, *The Jester.* However, it was almost inevitable that at some point during the evening I would run across Carlos. After the initial period of being nodding acquaintances which comes about through recognising familiar people, we eventually spoke and finally began to form a friendship. Whenever or wherever I met him, one thing one could guarantee, was that Carlos was always entertaining and amusing company.

Carlos was also genuinely interested in people. He not only knew many people but he also knew a lot about them. He knew about their loves, their lives, their occupations, their incomes and because he had been on the scene for so long he often knew intimate details of their sexual history having seen them in some cases grow from bright eyed young men and women to older more wiser men and women who had felt the backhand of life smack some sense into them. He shared their joys but also wept at their sorrows and sufferings.

Over a period of several years I began to know and become known on the Gay Scene, befriending some of the other well know characters like Phil MacDonald, who was a charismatic, outrageous, loud, and at times foul-mouthed Scot. Exchanges between Phil and Carlos made for wonderful side-splitting theatre shows. I also got to know the owner of *Missing* – 'Lady B' – who did a fabulous drag act, and came to enjoy the relaxed, friendly but always engaging atmosphere of the bar, and often spent time there.

Another friend I made at the time was Bill, a more thoughtful and gently spoken Scotsman, who was also good friends with Phil but temperamentally quite different. Bill and I used to meet in my other favourite haunt which was *The Green Room*. It was located at the top of Hurst Street and was not really a gay bar per se, but what was termed a 'gay-friendly establishment'. To me it was the perfect cafe bar, real wooden tables, a relaxed and friendly atmosphere and delicious, if somewhat pricey food. I often met Bill here and we would discuss philosophy, literature, politics, religion and poetry, and all before a drop of alcohol had touched our lips.

I believe it was through Bill that my interest in writing came to be known. On one of our meetings sometime in 2002 I shared with him some poems I had written about a boyfriend I had recently broken up with. The Birmingham Gay Scene being what it is and relatively small, I was taken aback but not I suppose, really surprised when the next time I met Phil, he greeted me as the 'Mad Poet'. Bill had shared the poems with him and the name stuck. Phil even entered me in his mobile phone as 'The Mad Poet'.

So, it was not really too surprising that one evening shortly after this, while Carlos and I were in the slow and chaotic process of getting drunk together that he floated the idea of me of writing his biography. This was crazy alcohol talk I decided. I tried to explain to Carlos that my interest in writing was for personal pleasure, and that apart from writing some poems, and a couple of over ambitious and pretentious verse plays, I had never attempted anything serious in prose. Nor was I really interested or equipped to write a biography. The matter was dropped and we returned to the alcohol.

Eventually this topic was to surface with recurring regularity at all our future meetings. Each time we met Carlos at some point during the evening would raise the issue of his biography even throwing in – as if in an attempt to entice me – the fact that Barbara Cartland had wanted to write it. Sadly, this was no great lure. My arrogance in attempting to align myself with the great poets of the past, meant that Barbara Cartland was viewed as a mere materialist and a commercial hack. Not that I had ever read any of her books but that did not matter. My own sense of superiority enabled me to dismiss her out of hand.

Carlos has, under the influence of alcohol, a tendency to be self-deprecating and self-indulgent. Often in the course of an evening together he would dip down into and wallow in a trough of self-pity. Tears would flow and Carlos would bemoan his existence, curse the sheer hardship of his life, regret his lack of love and the fact that he did not have a boyfriend, and that he was no longer able to enjoy the applause and adulation that his former lifestyle had brought him.

Clearly the biography of Carlos was not a project I was really interested in, nor had the confidence that I could even do. A poem is often only a few lines long, whereas a book may need to run to a hundred pages. Or more. However, I did sympathise with Carlos when he went into one of his rants against life, and the idea of doing something to help alleviate his suffering was always one that managed to touch my heart. In an effort to, at least throw him a small crumb of hope, I began to wonder what writing a biography would be like, and finally in June 2010 I wrote down the first idea I had for approaching such an undertaking. The first few paragraphs (printed in italics at the start of this chapter) were the first thing I wrote about Carlos' life. When I showed it to Carlos he was delighted by it. Insignificant though it was, it seemed to very quickly do the rounds of our mutual friends on the Gay Scene. This I found scary.

What started out as an attempt (if somewhat futile) to ease someone's suffering soon became a huge rod to beat myself with. Carlos seemed to think I was actually working on his biography and now when we met asked me how it was going. I began to feel guilty and wanted to be rid of this albatross that I had inadvertently hung around my neck. I spoke to another gay friend who was working hard developing himself as a novelist and whose work I greatly admired, and asked him if he would be interested in taking on this project. This went badly wrong as he and Carlos did not see eye to eye and that attempt failed miserably.

As time wore on I began to come to the conclusion that maybe I ought to take this project more seriously and actually begin to work out what would be required to write a biography. In this more positive vein I approach Carlos, making clear that I was only doing exploratory work, and that nothing might come of it. However, we agreed to meet up from time to time to and he would begin to tell me of his life.

The first few meetings were, from a writing point of view, complete disasters. Carlos had no idea of the writing process nor did he seem to have any sense of chronology. We met a few times in *The Village* at the bottom of Hurst Street as it tended to be a little quieter - certainly in the earlier hours of the evening. But new to this biography business myself, I foolishly did not take any notes, or record the conversation in any way, and was happy just to listen to what he had to say. Carlos would tell me of incidents that had happened earlier that week, mixed in with events which took place when he was a child, followed by something that happened in 1980 and so I was being deluged by a kaleidoscope of images, impressions anecdotes and encounters from his life but with no logical sequence to them. Coupled with this was the fact that we were both sat at a bar drinking and, as the evening wore on, we got drunker and drunker, until eventually I got a taxi home and Carlos vanished out into the night. The next morning I recalled nothing except vague, distorted remnants of the content of our discussion, and began to consider that this might not be the best way to proceed with such an undertaking.

It was to take several more of these abortive attempts before I finally came to the conclusion that one cannot really write a biography, or indeed engage in any form of literary endeavour, while in a state of increasing inebriation. So, I arranged for Carlos and I to meet in *The Green Room*, where I would turn up much more prepared, having thought through some questions I wanted to ask, and also now carrying a note-book with me in order to record the answers. This method proved much more successful. However, as if an indication of the daunting task that lay ahead, for our first meeting on the 1st August 2010 Carlos turned up over an hour late. There had been an incident and his bus had apparently been stopped by the police.

Carlos was not a literary man, and his life to him was much more visual and photographic. He soon lent me some of his photo albums, showing him during his career as an aerial contortionist, and my questions tended to focus on drawing out the incident and background to the pictured event. I also began to search for Carlos via the internet but that proved to be very unhelpful as there seemed to be very little about him available on the world-wide-web. However, I was able to research places where he lived and slowly and surely began to put a book outline together, constructing it more like a jig-saw puzzle than unwrapping it like a silk cloak.

After our meetings I would go off and write up the contents of our discussion and then arrange to meet Carlos, read what I had written to him, and ask for comments and corrections. This process seemed to work after a fashion but even this method had its draw backs. Despite it being a sizable venue *The Green Room*, was still very much a public space and people were constantly looking over or eavesdropping on our conversation. There was also the continuous battle with alcohol. (Note to self: don't go to a bar if you want to stay sober!)

On the 2nd September 2010, I had arranged to meet Carlos at 4.30 pm. Used to him not being very punctual, I was not too bothered when by 5 pm he had not turned up. I waited patiently a little longer.

By 5.15 pm I decided to phone him. Strangely enough Phil answered. It appeared that he and Carlos were only about 50 metres away down the road in *Missing*. Carlos had not recognised his phone's ring-tone and Phil had got fed up with the noise and answered it for him. Phil put Carlos on the phone and Carlos said he would be up shortly. I phoned again about 5.30 pm but by now he was even more drunk, so I went down to see him. As soon as I entered the bar it was clear that nothing was going to happen on the biography that day so I went home.

Around this time I began to keep an occasional journal of progress and this rather cryptic entry indicates yet another failed meeting:-

26th April 2011

Agee to meet up with Carlos in Green Room at 2pm. He does not show. I called him, he sounded drunk and in a pub. Said he would be 10 mins. I called again at 2.30 he said he was at the market on his way. At 3pm I left and had a look in Missing and the Village but could not see him. After looking in the Village I turned back up the street towards Missing. Carlos was in Missing when I looked in on my way back and we spoke briefly. He had lost 4 friends in one week (4 funerals) one a friend in Peru who was only 26 years old and had committed suicide. No bio today. Came home.

When I met Carlos after this he explained that the young man in Peru had committed suicide because he was gay and the persecution, ridicule and anti-gay prejudice he encountered made him feel that life was not worth living. This news had been particularly painful for Carlos to bear.

I think one of the most startling encounters I had with Carlos at this time happened late one afternoon as I was on my way home from work.

I often took to walking down Hurst Street, which served me as a short-cut to an alternative bus route home to use when the town had become gridlocked with congestion due to the volume of traffic. It was a pleasant warm summer afternoon and people were on their way home or catching up on some last-minute shopping. Hurst Street was still fairly quiet and the chairs outside *Missing* were still unoccupied. As the evening wore on they would fill to capacity and the currently muted noise from the bar would rise to a crescendo as people began to *party on down*!

I had just gone past and was about ten to fifteen metres away when I heard a voice. "Mr John! Mr John!" I turned in time to see Carlos hurtle drunkenly out of the *Missing* doorway and stagger sideways into the middle of road. He was wearing a bright yellow patterned Hawaiian shirt which was open down to his waist and flapping around his arms in the light warm breeze. I stopped in my tracks and took in this unholy apparition. He continued to stand in the middle of road waving at me, so I decided for the sake of road-safety if for no other reason, to go back up the street and talk to him. He was delighted to see me and explained he had managed to find some more photographs for me. We stood there for several minutes with the traffic trying to negotiate its way around us as I tried to get him to move back to the pavement. Eventually I succeeded. As we stood there in relative safety Carlos tried to persuade me to join him at the bar. After a further five or ten minutes I managed to convince him that I was very tired after my days' work and needed to get home for something to eat. After asking if I could lend him £20, which I could, we agreed to part and I headed on down Hurst Street glancing back just in time to see Carlos burst flamboyantly and drunkenly back into the semi-empty bar.

There were times when writing the biography was hell. After I had written the first draft of the first chapter Carlos and I joked about how rich we would become. I explained to him that even if I could ever find a publisher, I would probably not earn any money from the book sales but suspected that he could probably earn a fortune doing interviews on the various TV talk shows where guests are invited to talk about their lives. This made Carlos feel happy and we both joked about becoming millionaires. Unfortunately, the more time went by the more I felt guilty about letting Carlos down. I realised that I did not have the skills or ability to carry such a project off and it came to represent a huge burden that I wanted to be rid of.

As luck would have it I stumbled across another means of learning about Carlos after buying a web-camera. For a project I did at college, I had to interview some people and used a web-cam to record the interview onto my computer and then typed it up afterwards. I arranged to visit Carlos at his house on the 20th August 2013 to see if this method of interviewing and recording would work.

As I was coming from work I'd told Carlos I would be there about 4 – 4.30 pm as I was unsure how long it would take. After a short bus ride I disembarked near Carlos' flat. On checking my phone I found I had a missed call. I had not heard it ring on the bus and it had gone straight to voicemail. In a strange irony, it was Carlos informing me that it was 4pm and that he was waiting!

Carlos lived in a ground floor flat, although in reality it was actually situated some several metres off the ground, situated in a very modern and purpose-built block of flats, run by a well-respected Birmingham Housing association. A few minutes later I was at the external intercom pressing the 'call' button. Nothing happened for several minutes and then Carlos appeared, pulling open the solid-looking wooden fire door which led to the glass-surrounded entry where I was waiting. He was wearing a white vest under a loose, light summer t-shirt affair, one half of which was white the other black, wide flowing white trousers and all capped off with some white canvas shoes. (Was there something bridal in all this symbolism?) He seemed pleased to see me and his large solid square face beamed a cheeky welcoming smile at me. With a flourish he let me into the block, and I followed him down the corridors through further fire doors and into his flat.

The wooden floors in the flat clacked loudly as my hard work-shoes tapped the resonate surface, sounding like a slightly out of sync Fred Astaire. I was struck by how low the ceilings were as I looked round at the coats and other items that hung in the hallway. Off to my right was the bathroom, while straight ahead lay the bedroom, to the side of which was what may have been a small second bedroom or a box room. Carlos directed me to the right and into the square living room which was lit by the light of a large window looking out onto one of busiest roads in the city. However, the planners had been clever and the flat was set back some way from the road and also elevated so one was almost level with the top deck of the many double-decker buses that passed.

Carlos was clearly excited and jokingly informed me he had been up since 7 am cleaning the flat. He had even borrowed a steam cleaner to get to those hard to reach places. I took a seat on the sofa, and began to set up my computer and web-camera, while Carlos disappeared into the kitchen to make some tea. He was always a very entertaining and hospitable host.

While he busied himself in the kitchen I took a minute to look round the room. On the wall that held the window, and the wall behind the couch I sat on, there were lots of framed black and white pictures of Carlos from his circus days, and even what appeared to be an oil portrait of him looking very fit and muscular; a signed picture of Barbara Cartland in the inevitable pink dress, along with three black and white photos of Marlene Dietrich one of which was signed. The opposite wall contained some bizarre paintings, one showing a whole collection of famous Hollywood films stars (including John Wayne) in what seemed to be some kind of reference to a picture from the Moulin Rouge period of Toulouse-Lautrec: a traditional still-life with fruit and flowers which looked Dutch, and some further portraits and photos I did not recognise.

The room also contained a table with four chairs, a television, and some other smaller pieces of furniture including a small glass table upon which sat a few pot-plants, and various knick-knacks, a collection of mugs commemorating various 'significant' events. At the back of these items was a picture, or possibly a promotional poster, of a lady called 'La Sylvia' provocatively attired in red leather boots, a skimpy two-piece red swimming suit and a small red leather jacket. She was holding a cross-bow, and therefore could have been involved in the circus in some way. In the bottom right of the frame a smaller picture had been inserted showing her dressed more soberly with, I presumed, her family. On a glass table under the window lay some books and magazines, some opened and neatly piled utility bills and letters and various pictures of Carlos in his prime. To the left of this stood a wavy plastic stand holding a collection of music CDs.

Carlos was still busy in the small but functional kitchen which seemed to be fitted with everything he required. Above the cooker he had displayed a collection of ornate plates including a large willow pattern serving platter. He moved back into the Living Room carrying a mug of hot tea and a side plate containing a very generous slice of cake. These were welcome gifts at the end of my working day.

After a few minutes more chit chat, I asked Carlos to sit opposite me on one of the dining chairs while I adjusted the camera to focus on his head and shoulders. I also managed to move some spotlights which he had on a stand by the door, and adjusted them so they would throw more light on his face. The radio was playing very low in the back ground. And we began. Carlos seemed very confident as he sat facing me and addressing my questions in a very frank and sometimes matter of fact way. He looked very commanding and regal. Suddenly I really could believe him when he said he had only felt nervous twice in his life. He seemed incredibly comfortable with the whole interview process and appeared able to recall dates, times, people and places as if they had only just happened. Most of the time he was very serious, but occasionally he would make a rude camp comment, or a cheeky aside, and we would dissolve in laughter. Sometimes too he would get so emotional that he would have to struggle hard to hold back his tears. And so, we went on...

These interviews were a very intimate affair and often proved an emotional rollercoaster for Carlos: joyful as he recalled the good times of his circus triumphs and the famous people he had met, sad, bitter and painful when he recalled times when he had been badly treated either by his family or by others. From time to time he would slip into moments of self-pity bemoaning his lot: why had he never been loved and why had he ended up so poor? Referring to his flat he spoke of it as a 'Grand chocolate box palace', meaning it was small and cramped. Then, as quickly as he had fallen into this Dantesque inferno of self-pity and pain, he would shake himself out of it, and rise back up to the heights, countering his depression with a list of the positive things that he had been blessed with: his health, his friends on the gay scene, his gratitude to Billy Arata and Margaret Hampson, and his flat. We would proceed in this emotional wave-like fashion every time.

Despite the details revealed in the interview, after I had transcribed them and begun to weave them into a chapter, I always discovered that they had produced even more questions than they answered, or revealed new aspects of his life that needed more clarity. It was like watching a TV mystery unfold. New clues led to new discoveries and took the story off in new and unexpected directions. The next time we met I would have to begin with a list of questions the previous interview had exposed.

However, this method had proved a clear winner and, with my now renewed connection to it, the book began to take shape and to grow at such a rate that for the first time since it began over four years before I could finally begin to believe that the project would actually come to an end.

Chapter 17

LIFE NOW!

Despite not having performed professionally since 1989, Carlos still manages to grab the limelight from time to time. The housing association, Optima, in one of whose properties Carlos resides, held a portrait project in 2009. The following year 2010, Optima showed the photographs from Sept – October, 2010 - at the local arts venue, *The MAC,* under the title 'Faces of Attwood Green'. One of the portraits featured was, of course, Carlos. The Optima magazine, 'Say Optima!' (Sept/Oct 2010) carries a short advertising notice for the event which features a picture of Carlos, looking very smart and 'normal' in a suit and tie, standing in front of his portrait which shows him wearing an outrageous tightly fitting jacket, whose multi-coloured diamond motif makes him look very like a Picasso jester, this atop a pair of tight fitting black, bell-bottom trousers which picked up the multi-coloured diamond motive again at the knees, and all topped off with an elaborate and outlandish feather hat!

As I write this, Carlos is now 68 years old and has reached that time in his life, and the time that most older people come to experience, when attending funerals becomes the norm. Very regularly Carlos gets news of departed friends from all across the world. Where he is able to, Carlos attends funerals, certainly the one's which are held in the UK, which are both a chance to get out, but also a stark reminder of his own mortality.

Over the last few years Carlos' health has deteriorated and at one point he was in a terribly anxious state as some tests revealed that there was the possibility that he had cancer. Further, more elaborate tests, put him in the clear, but it was a difficult and painful few weeks. At that time his Doctor was also very concerned about his level of drinking. Although, when relating this account, Carlos puts a rather funny, if not completely true, spin on it. After the tests, the Doctor had expressed grave concern about the level of alcohol Carlos had in his system. When Carlos asked if he would have to give up drinking, the Doctor did a double-take and in a shocked and quavering voice replied, "No! for God's sake no!" Then adding, as if in the form of an explanation, that it was probably the alcohol that was preserving his organs and that stopping drinking would most probably kill him!

Carlos also gets very lonely, as he said at one of the interviews I conducted:

Sometimes I cry a lot when I here on my own. I get very lonely. Why am I so unlucky, why do I not have a lover? I am so lonely, so sad. Then again people say to me there are a lot of people who are not lucky like you. You have a roof over your head. You live in the middle of the City of Birmingham. When you don't have any money we don't mind, we buy you drinks. When we don't have money, and you have money, you don't mind, you buy us drinks.

However, the reciprocity of alcoholism only goes so far. As we have seen Carlos is normally able quickly to lift himself out of such bouts of self-loathing, but the area that hurts him the most, is that associated with being loved. We have seen that from an early age Carlos suffered mental and physical abuse and that the lithe, white, angelic vision of his circus spirit helped carry him well beyond that early suffering, indeed gave him the means to climb and soar above it (both literally and metaphorically). But we have often seen that from time to time he would fall. Fall to the earth with a crashing, smashing, thud, and damage himself even more. Carlos was always looking for love, looking for someone to take him in his arms and call him his own. For many years that love was provided by the satisfied and elated audiences after his performances, but after Cologne that source of love was no longer available. Yes, he could go out on the gay scene and perform, and he did, and for a while that was a source of joy, a source of satisfaction, but ultimately it could never replace the love he sought. Nothing could.

> *"All the world used her ill, said this young misanthropist, and we may be pretty certain that persons whom all the world treats ill, deserve entirely the treatment they get. The world is a looking -glass, and gives back to every man the reflection of his own face. Frown at it, and it will in turn look sourly upon you; laugh at it and with it, and it is a jolly kind companion; and so let all young persons take their choice."*

> *(Vanity Fair - William Makepeace Thackeray).*

From 1985 onwards, although Carlos chose to abstain from Sex, after seeing the effect of the AIDS virus, which had then begun to run rampant over the planet, it did not absolve him from having to deal with the problems and diseases of the heart. On occasions when we spoke about his love-life Carlos always seemed to be very philosophical and would say, "Vanity Fair. Vanity Fair. Vanity Fair."

At the time I completely misunderstood this reference and thought Carlos was referring to William Makepeace Thackeray's novel which is a satirical panorama of a materialistic society, where we view the lives of the characters rather as if we observed them in a play. The intertwining love stories, the pursuit of wealth and power and the cheating and betrayals all seem too familiar. However, for Carlos, the Vanity Fair he had in mind was the glitzy American gossip, fashion magazine, which deals with the loves and lives of the rich and famous, the stars of the world of fashion and of Hollywood movies. So, although I misunderstood his reference they do both deal with fleeting unreal and unsatisfactory worlds, where the only constant winner is suffering and the only character to triumph is Death itself.

Carlos, like us all, is aware of the false attractions of the material world, and the lure of romantic, and idealized love, fragile and brittle though it is, but it does not stop either us or him from wanting it, nay from actively seeking it, from time to time. For Carlos, the search for a meaningful love goes on. However, given his age and the knowledge that so many of his friends are dying around him, there is now a sense of urgency and an edge of desperation in Carlos' quest. Feelings of bitterness and rage rise to the surface and sometimes cause him to lash out, striking at those he most wants to hold tightly. Jealousy rages through him untrammelled, resulting in him literally spitting out his feelings of venom. Recently his outrageous behaviour has resulted in him being banned from certain pubs. As Oscar Wilde said in *The Ballad of Reading Gaol,*'...each man kills the thing he loves' and Carlos is no exception.

Speaking of a recent and particularly painful unrequited love affair that he was still in the throes of, Carlos recounted to me that he was, 'in love from his heart.' He spoke about it being a beautiful situation, and producing a wonderful sensation. "Being is love is like being on a magic carpet, you feel wonderful inside. It's fabulous." However, he was also aware enough to know of the dangerous seas it could steer you into. "But it's also sad, painful, evil, and nasty. It's very painful. It ruins your life. The other side of love is extreme. You think about killing yourself. You think about killing the person you are in love with because that person does not want you."

During December 2013 Carlos became very ill and was confined to his flat. The Doctor was visiting him daily and prescribing a large selection of pills because his blood pressure was too high, he was having trouble urinating, and when he was able to urinate there was often blood in it. The Doctor was concerned about his liver too. Despite these rather serious symptoms Carlos seemed more concerned about this recent love affair, or more correctly his recent infatuation. Clearly for someone like Carlos, who was denied so much love throughout his life, he was desperate to grasp and cling onto whatever morsels of love and affection that he could, regardless that it was totally unrequited. It seemed, certainly in Carlos' mind, that his current state of ill health was linked directly to his lack of love.

Reflecting on the infatuation Carlos again become philosophical. In a phrase reminiscent of the famous, 'It's China town', line from the classic Jack Nicholson movie 'Chinatown', Carlos said, "That's what happens when you go out on the gay scene." Such it seems are the machinations of love. We fall in love with people who are unattainable, or who do not even notice our existence, while at the same time doing exactly the same thing to those who want to get close to us.

Carlos was clearly going through the process of trying to deal with his recent hurt and pain by trying to convince himself that he was not deluding himself. "I am not dreaming a Babylonian dream", he said. Speaking of the boy in question he added, "I only want to be his friend. I would be very happy to make him a sandwich, or a cup of tea or cocoa. But nothing more." Continuing in the same vein, and pontificating like the reformed character of a Victorian novel, Carlos began to argue very cogently, in a somewhat desperate and contradictory way, in an attempt to convince himself of the value and the moral benefits of his new abstinent position.

The emotions within him were rising and falling like the turbulent and troubled waves on a storm beaten cliff. Someone had suggested erroneously to the young man in question that Carlos was going to kill himself over his unrequited love for him. In recounting this to me the white spume of the crashing waves spat like venom from his lips. Carlos was almost apoplectic. "I was in love with him, but why would I want to kill myself for him? When he's out on the piss he'll not be thinking about me! If I did kill myself, all he'd think is, 'Why did that old piss artist kill himself for me? He'd think, I'd rather have cock (sex) than heart (love). That's the attitude of the younger generation!' For me, I would rather just be friends."

There was a long pause, and the fury of the storm began to abate. Vanishing as quickly as it had arisen. So fickle is the heart of man. And such is the turmoil in the breast of the hero of our tale. Despite the extraordinary achievements of his early life in the Circus it seems we are all at the mercy of our emotions. Like us all, Carlos is haunted and plagued by the pains and the joys of love. And like Thackeray's looking-glass, the world has reflected back a range of faces: joys and triumphs, as well as desperation, loneliness and self-indulgence, but Carlos soldiers on. Catching himself sliding down the steep slope towards the depths of despair he seems able to quickly arrest his fall, with a cheeky joke, or a self-deprecating comment.

For Carlos, turbulent though it is, life goes on...

ACKNOWLEDGMENTS

Clearly the main acknowledgement must go to Carlos in allowing me – to the best of my ability - to write his story. It was told to me in a somewhat random and haphazard manner and I hope there are not too many occasions where my imagination has taken a random comment, or description of an event and supplanted the truth.

The photographs in this book are unattributed and all belong to Carlos. I understand that they were taken by his friends and then given to him. He in turn has given me permission to use them.

Thanks, must go to Roland Van Halst, from Circus Net who helped me gather information from various circus programmes that featured Carlos.

http://www.circusnet.info/index.php?locale=en

I would like to thank Francisco Dominguez-Montero for translating articles about contortionism from Spanish newspapers which Carlos lent me as background information; Phil McDonald who very kindly supplied me with a scanner at the start of this process when I needed such a device to capture the photographs that Carlos held so dear; to Timm Sonnenschein, who re-imaged the photos for use in this book; and to the staff at Circus Report for permission to use information from their helpful publication:

http://www.thecircusreport.com/index.html

Finally, I'd like to record a debt of gratitude to my friend Chris Clinton for his support throughout the long drawn out writing of this book and for taking the time to read through it for mistakes. Needless to say any errors or omissions are totally my own.

John Wright

NON-FICTION FROM APS BOOKS
www.andrewsparke.com

Aramoana (Andrew Sparke)
Bella In The Wych-Elm (Andrew Sparke)
Countdown Cath (Cathy Hytner)
Croc Curry & Texas Tea: Surviving Nigeria (Paul Dickinson)
Diana Rigg Ruined My Life (Chris Grayling)
Eye 2i (Paul Sorensen)
Glimpses Into Sutton's Past 1800-1914 (Stephen Roberts)
Indie Publishing: The Journey Made Easy (Andrew Sparke)
Istanbul: The Visitor Essentials (Andrew Sparke)
Leaving Lewis (Helen Pitt)
Magna Carta Wars Of Lincoln Cathedral (Andrew Sparke)
More Swings Than Roundabouts (John Wright)
Piggery Jokery In Tonga (Andrew Sparke)
Rear Gunner (Andrew Sparke)
Stutthof (Andrew Sparke)
Tales From Pinfold Farm (Helen Pitt)
The Devil's Cauldron (Pete Merrill)
The Erstwhile Buddhist (Helen Pitt)
The Strange Free-Fall Of Fred Ryland (Helen Pitt)
The Ways Of Mevagissey (Andrew Sparke)
Travels With My Tuba (Jim Anderson)
War Shadows (Andrew Sparke)
Who Put Bella In The Wych Elm? Vol.1 The Crime Scene Revisited (Alex Merrill)
Who Put Bella In The Wych Elm? Vol.2 A Crime Shrouded In Mystery (Alex Merrill)